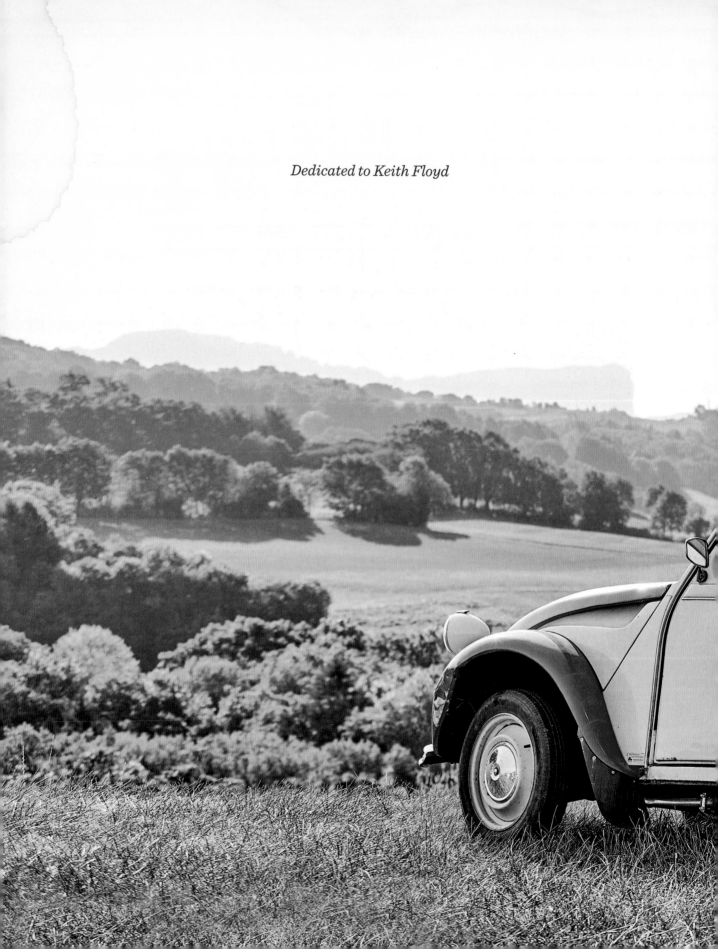

Dedicated to Keith Floyd

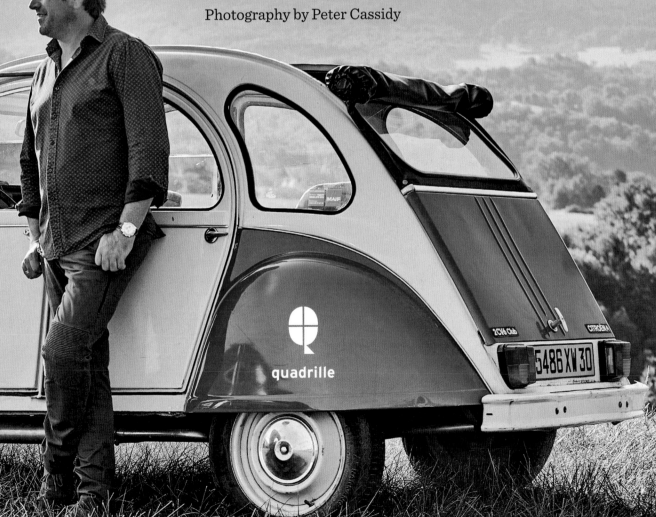

JAMES MARTIN'S
— FRENCH —
ADVENTURE

Photography by Peter Cassidy

quadrille

Publishing director: Sarah Lavelle
Creative director: Helen Lewis
Art direction and design: Smith & Gilmour
Photography: Peter Cassidy
Senior editor: Lisa Pendreigh
Project editor: Alison Cowan
Food preparation and styling:
James Martin, Sam Head and Chris Start
Props stylist: Iris Bromet
Home economists: Sam Head and Louise Pickford
Production: Emily Noto and Vincent Smith

The publishers would like to thank Gill and Jon at Sytch Farm
Studios for the generous loan of props for the photography.

First published in 2017 by Quadrille Publishing
Pentagon House, 52–54 Southwark Street, London SE1 1UN

Quadrille Publishing is an imprint of Hardie Grant
www.hardiegrant.com.au
www.quadrille.co.uk   www.quadrille.com

Reprinted in 2017
10 9 8 7 6 5 4 3 2

Text © 2017 James Martin
Photography © 2017 Peter Cassidy
Design and layout © 2017 Quadrille Publishing

Cataloguing in Publication Data: a catalogue record
for this book is available from the British Library.

ISBN: 978 1 84949 954 5

Printed in Germany

INTRODUCTION

Why France, you might ask, and why now?

Well, it's been over thirty-five years since I went there as a young chef and, in a way, I owe it all to France. I mean, it was those early trips that set the course of my career – from the unforgettable taste of my first croissant to seeing a steak cooked 'blue', not burnt to a cinder.

Back then it wasn't easy training as a chef in France, but I was there for a reason, and I could put up with the nineteen-hour days peeling veg in the kitchen of a Michelin two-starred restaurant, and head chefs giving me grief, as long as I got to learn about food. For me, it's always been about the food; everything else comes second.

While I'd wanted to go back for a long time – to see what had changed, and to taste again the food that had changed me – ultimately what triggered this TV series and book was a phone call from Keith Floyd's daughter, Poppy. She wanted to know if I'd be interested in her dad's old car, his much-loved Citroën 2CV. My answer was never really in any doubt, and seventy-two hours later a battered and bruised 2CV was in my garage. Even better, it had been left untouched and smelt like a spit bucket at Oddbins, a heady combination of musk and good Burgundy. Best of all, it now took pride of place in my garage, providing the inspiration for a very special road trip.

Like most people, I first came across Keith Floyd on TV. But it wasn't long before our paths crossed in real life. While I was at catering college, he came to host a gourmet evening for a hundred and fifty people, and I was one of the students in the kitchen. I remember he was supposed to stand up between courses to announce each dish – but, Keith being Keith, right at the beginning of the meal he strode up to the lectern, uttered a few words to introduce all of us eager young cooks to the room and then promptly fell off the stage!

Now, as a TV chef myself, I've been lucky enough to cook with some of the best chefs in the world, but if you asked me to name the greatest of all the TV chefs, I'd have to say Keith Floyd. For me, the three-minute clip of him battling the elements on the deck of a fishing trawler has never been beaten: it was all done in one take, and he nearly swore three times. It's still one of the best TV cookery moments ever, and one I find myself watching time and time again.

Having been in this game for more than twenty years now, I know how difficult it can be, and how easy he made it all look. He never pretended to be anything other than what he was: a man with a passion for food and for life, and with a talent that was enjoyed by so many.

Some thirty years since *Floyd on France* first screened, the chance to follow in his footsteps, and to return to the places that have shaped my own life and career, was too good to resist. I hope this book will give you a small taste of what I learnt and the things I discovered on my French adventure, and that you'll enjoy the trip as much as I did. One thing's for sure, it won't be another thirty-odd years before I head back.

SNACKS, SOUPS & STARTERS

This amazing cheese cellar in the Jura mountains was stacked floor to ceiling with huge wheels of Comté – and there's now one with my name on it that I'll be going back to collect when it matures in around three years' time.

COMTÉ CHOUX PUFFS

MAKES TWENTY

115g butter
200g plain flour
1 teaspoon caster sugar
pinch of salt
4 eggs
200g Comté cheese, grated
1 teaspoon paprika

Preheat the oven to 200°C/400°F/gas mark 6. Line a baking tray with baking parchment.

Heat the butter with 250ml water in a saucepan over medium heat until the butter has melted. Add the flour, sugar and salt all at once and, using a wooden spoon, beat well until smooth. Continue to cook for 1–2 minutes, still stirring, until the mixture comes away from the sides of the pan. Remove from the heat and leave to cool slightly for a minute or two, then beat in the eggs, one at a time, until the mixture is smooth and glossy. Stir in the cheese and paprika.

Set aside to cool, then spoon the dough into a piping bag fitted with a medium-sized plain nozzle. Pipe 5cm rounds onto the prepared baking tray, spacing them well apart. Bake for 20 minutes until puffed up, golden and crispy. Serve warm with drinks.

SPICY WALNUTS

SERVES FOUR

125g butter
150g brown sugar
1 teaspoon cayenne pepper
300g walnut halves
1 egg white

Preheat the oven to 160°C/325°F/gas mark 3. Line a baking tray with baking parchment.

Place the butter and sugar in a frying pan and heat gently until the butter has melted. Increase the heat and cook, stirring, for 3–4 minutes until the sugar has dissolved to make a caramel. Stir in the cayenne pepper, then fold in the walnuts. Remove from the heat.

Whisk the egg white to stiff peaks, then fold gently into the walnut mixture until the nuts are evenly coated. Transfer the walnuts to the prepared baking tray and cook for 15–20 minutes, stirring every 6–8 minutes, until the nuts are golden and crisp. Leave to cool before serving with drinks, on a cheeseboard or to add crunch to salads.

Fresh, simple and tasty, this soup can be made with any vegetables you like
– just be careful not to overcook them, so they retain their colour.

PISTOU SOUP

10 plum tomatoes
100g frozen broad beans
4 tablespoons extra virgin
  olive oil
1 onion, finely chopped
1 garlic clove, finely chopped
1 leek, cut into small dice
1 medium carrot, cut into
  small dice
1 courgette, cut into small dice
2 medium potatoes, peeled
  and cut into small dice
75g green beans, topped
  and tailed and cut into
  3cm lengths
75g spaghetti
100g frozen peas
400g tin haricot beans,
  drained and rinsed
200g bacon lardons
sea salt and freshly ground
  black pepper

For the pistou
60g basil leaves
1 garlic clove, peeled but
  left whole
75g freshly grated Parmesan
100ml extra virgin olive oil

Cut a small cross into the base of each tomato and place in a heatproof bowl. Add boiling water to cover and leave for 2–3 minutes until the tomato skins start to peel away. Drain, then refresh under cold water and peel completely. Cut in half, then scoop out and discard the seeds. Set one of the tomatoes aside and dice the rest.

Bring a small saucepan of water to the boil, add the broad beans and blanch for 1 minute. Drain, refresh under cold water and shake dry. Peel and discard the outer shell. Set the beans aside.

Heat a large saucepan over medium heat, add 3 tablespoons of the olive oil and fry the onion, garlic, leek, carrot, courgette and potatoes for 5 minutes. Add the green beans, along with enough water to cover, and bring to the boil.

Wrap the spaghetti in a clean tea towel and roll it across the edge of a worktop, pressing backwards and forwards to break it into small pieces. Add to the soup with the diced tomatoes and simmer for 10 minutes to cook the pasta. Add the peas, broad beans and haricot beans and heat through for 4 minutes.

While the soup is cooking, make the pistou. Place all the ingredients in a food processor, along with the reserved tomato, and blend to a pesto-like texture.

Heat a small frying pan over medium heat, add the remaining tablespoon of olive oil and sauté the bacon lardons until crisp.

Remove the soup from the heat, stir in the lardons and season well. Ladle into bowls, add a spoonful of pesto and serve straightaway.

FRENCH ONION SOUP
WITH CHEESY CROÛTONS

SERVES FOUR

25g butter
2 tablespoons olive oil
1kg white onions, finely sliced
2 sprigs of thyme, leaves picked
3 garlic cloves, finely chopped
50ml dry sherry
250ml white wine
2 tablespoons plain flour
1.2 litres veal or beef stock
1 teaspoon soft brown sugar
sea salt and freshly ground
   black pepper
1 small baguette, thickly
   sliced on the diagonal
110g Gruyère cheese, grated

Heat a large sauté pan until hot. Add the butter and oil and fry the onions and thyme for 20–25 minutes over low to medium heat, stirring from time to time, until softened and golden brown. Add the garlic and cook for another couple of minutes.

Add the sherry and white wine and simmer until reduced by half. Stir in the flour and cook for 1 minute, stirring constantly. Stir in the stock, a little at a time, then bring to a simmer and cook gently for 15 minutes. Season with the sugar, salt and pepper.

Meanwhile, preheat the grill to high. Toast the baguette slices lightly on each side. Sprinkle the cheese onto the toasts and return to the grill until bubbling and golden brown.

Ladle the soup into bowls and top with the cheesy croûtons.

You'll need to start this comforting soup a day ahead, as the split peas must be soaked overnight.

SPLIT PEA SOUP
WITH BAYONNE HAM

SERVES FOUR

2 tablespoons olive oil
2 shallots, diced
200g yellow split peas,
    soaked overnight
500ml chicken stock
200ml double cream
4 slices Bayonne ham
sea salt and freshly
    ground black pepper

Heat the oil in a saucepan and fry the shallots over medium heat for 1–2 minutes until starting to soften.

Drain the soaked peas, then add to the pan with the chicken stock and bring to the boil. Simmer gently for 25–30 minutes, or until the peas are soft. Remove from the heat.

Using a stick blender, blend the soup until smooth. Stir in the cream and season to taste with salt and pepper, then gently reheat the soup to warm through.

Ladle the soup into bowls and top with the Bayonne ham.

In markets and supermarkets right across France, I found bucket-loads of these knobbly artichokes. You won't know how good they taste until you try them – they're ace! Once they're peeled, just remember to keep them in a bowl of cold water and lemon juice if you're not cooking them straightaway or they'll start to go brown.

JERUSALEM ARTICHOKE SOUP

SERVES FOUR

25ml olive oil
2 shallots, diced
400g Jerusalem
   artichokes, peeled
   and roughly chopped
50ml anise liqueur,
   such as Pernod
100ml white wine
25ml brandy
300ml chicken stock
200ml double cream
sea salt and freshly
   ground black pepper
warm crusty bread,
   to serve

Heat the olive oil in a large non-stick saucepan and fry the shallots and artichokes over medium heat for 5 minutes until the shallots are soft but not browned.

Add the anise liqueur, wine and brandy and cook for 1 minute. Pour in the chicken stock and bring to the boil, then turn down to a simmer and cook for 20–25 minutes until the artichokes are tender.

Transfer the soup to a blender (or use a stick blender) and blitz until smooth. Pass the soup through a fine sieve into a clean saucepan and stir in the cream. Season to taste with salt and pepper, then heat gently for 2–3 minutes until warmed through.

Pour the soup into bowls and serve with warm crusty bread.

Ceps (also called porcini) are probably the most common wild mushrooms in France, and are often available fresh in autumn. If you can't get hold of any, try making this delicious tart with chestnut mushrooms instead.

CEP TART

SERVES SIX

For the pastry
200g plain flour
¼ teaspoon salt
100g cold unsalted
  butter, diced
1 egg, beaten
1 teaspoon lemon juice
2 tablespoons iced water

For the filling
25g butter
2 shallots, finely diced
250g fresh ceps, wiped
  clean and sliced
4 eggs
200ml double cream
sea salt and freshly
  ground black pepper

To make the pastry, sift the flour and salt into a bowl and add half the butter. Using your fingertips, gently and swiftly rub the butter into the flour until it resembles coarse breadcrumbs. Add the rest of the butter and rub in until the mixture starts to form clumps the size of small peas. Make a well in the centre of the dry ingredients.

In a small bowl, mix together the beaten egg, lemon juice and water, then gradually pour into the dry ingredients, a little at a time, using a knife to help form a dough – you may not need all the liquid. Turn out the dough onto a floured board and knead lightly until smooth. Shape into a ball, wrap in cling film and refrigerate for at least 30 minutes.

Preheat the oven to 200°C/400°F/gas mark 6. Roll out the pastry on a lightly floured surface to a 5mm thickness and carefully press into a 22cm tart tin, leaving the edges hanging over. Line the pastry case with baking parchment, fill with dried beans or rice and blind bake for about 15 minutes until the pastry is set.

Meanwhile, for the filling, melt the butter in a large non-stick frying pan until foaming and fry the shallots and ceps for 4–5 minutes until deep golden brown.

Remove the tart case from the oven and lift out the baking paper and beans, then trim the overhanging pastry edges.

Whisk the eggs and cream together in a bowl, season with salt and pepper and pour into the tart case. Gently and evenly spoon in the cep mixture, then bake the tart for 25–30 minutes until golden and set.

Wherever you go in France, at most neighbourhood cafés and restaurants you'll be served a simple terrine like this, either cooked in a terrine mould or just in a bowl.

PORK, PISTACHIO & APRICOT TERRINE

SERVES EIGHT TO TEN

For the terrine
900g good-quality pork sausages
250g dried apricots, chopped
250g pistachios
150g pitted black olives, chopped
10g flat-leaf parsley, finely
  chopped
1 egg, lightly beaten
a little olive oil
450g streaky bacon rashers,
  rind removed
sea salt and freshly ground
  black pepper

For the chutney
30g butter
12 dark-skinned plums, stones
  removed and flesh chopped
6 tablespoons caster sugar
6 tablespoons balsamic vinegar
1 cinnamon stick

To serve
crusty bread

First make the terrine. Using a sharp knife, cut the skin from the sausages and squeeze out the filling into the bowl of an electric mixer. Start mixing at low speed, adding the apricots, pistachios, olives, parsley and beaten egg. When everything is well combined, season with salt and pepper. To check the seasoning, simply fry a small spoonful of the mixture in a pan until cooked, then taste and adjust the seasoning as needed.

Preheat the oven to 160°C/325°F/gas mark 3 and brush a large lidded terrine mould with olive oil. Use the streaky bacon to line the mould, allowing a slight overlap in the base and leaving 4cm overhanging the mould on both sides.

Spoon a few tablespoons of the terrine mixture into the base of the mould and press down well – this will prevent any air bubbles forming. Spoon in the rest of the mixture, again pressing down well. Fold the overhanging rashers of bacon over the top of the terrine and brush the underside of the lid with a little oil before placing firmly on the top. Place the terrine in a roasting tin and carefully pour in enough hot water to come half way up the side of the mould. Place in the oven and cook for 1¼–1½ hours, or until a skewer inserted into the centre comes out clean. Remove the terrine from the oven, carefully lift it out of the water bath and allow to cool completely before chilling in the fridge overnight.

For the chutney, melt the butter in a heavy-based frying pan and sauté the plums over medium heat for 2–3 minutes. Add the sugar, vinegar and cinnamon and simmer for 15–20 minutes until the plums are soft and the sauce is rich and sticky. Leave to cool.

To serve, simply turn the terrine out of the mould and serve with the chutney and some crusty bread. I like to slice it at the table and let people help themselves.

For some reason, the producers decided I should cook this standing in the middle of a river, with my trousers rolled up to my knees. The location bore absolutely no relation to what I was cooking – but, to be fair, it was stunning, and so is this dish (pictured over the page).

CONFIT DUCK ROSTI
WITH FRIED HEN'S EGG

SERVES TWO

3 waxy potatoes, such
  as Charlotte, peeled
2 tablespoons crème fraîche
2 sprigs of thyme, leaves picked
3 eggs
1 confit duck leg (see page 120)
  or 1 tinned confit duck leg,
  plus a little extra duck fat
8 slices fresh black truffle or a
  drizzle of truffle oil (optional)
sea salt and freshly ground
  black pepper

Grate the potatoes over a clean tea towel, then fold up the towel and squeeze out any excess water. Put the squeezed potato in a bowl and add the crème fraîche and thyme. Lightly beat one of the eggs and stir into the mixture, then season with salt and pepper and set aside.

Take the confit duck leg and pull off the meat, keeping the duck fat that covers the leg but discarding the bones and skin. Flake the duck meat and stir into the potato mixture.

Place the duck fat in a small saucepan, heat gently until it melts then remove from the heat. Drizzle just enough of the duck fat into a heavy-based frying pan to cover the base of the pan and place over medium heat. Add the truffle slices or oil, if using, to the remaining fat in the saucepan and set aside to infuse while you cook the rosti and eggs.

Divide the potato mixture in half and spoon into the frying pan to form 2 patties. Fry over medium heat for 3–4 minutes. When the edges start to go golden brown, turn them over and fry for a further 3–4 minutes until the rosti are cooked through. Transfer to warmed plates and keep warm.

Crack the 2 remaining eggs into the frying pan and fry for about 2–3 minutes until cooked to your liking. Place an egg on top of each rosti, drizzle over a little of the truffle-infused duck fat and finish with sliced truffle, if using. Serve immediately.

Venturing through the markets in France, I found lots of anchovies in jars and tins – just the thing for this anchovy dip. Gently heat the dip and serve it warm for a more mellow flavour. I like to serve this with a bunch of very fresh radishes with their leaves left on, or a selection of colourful vegetables.

CRUDITÉS
WITH ANCHOVY DIP

SERVES SIX TO EIGHT

2 heads red chicory,
  leaves separated
1 bunch of French breakfast
  radishes, washed
2 red peppers, cored and sliced
200g cherry tomatoes

For the anchovy dip
4 x 30g tins of anchovies, drained
1 lemon, zested
1 garlic clove, crushed
75ml double cream
75ml olive oil
freshly ground black pepper

To make the anchovy dip, place the anchovies, lemon zest, garlic and cream in a food processor and blitz until smooth. With the motor running, slowly drizzle in the olive oil until the sauce is thick and smooth. Season with pepper.

Pour the dip into a small bowl and serve with the vegetables.

Rillettes can be made with shredded duck, chicken or rabbit, and are one of the most delicious things you can have on toast, as the fat the rillettes are cooked in melts into the warm bread. Served with a deeply flavoured fruit chutney, this is proper French food.

DUCK RILLETTES
WITH FIG & PEACH CHUTNEY

SERVES FOUR

For the chutney
100g caster sugar
100g dried figs, diced
50g sultanas
2 peaches, stones removed
    and flesh diced
1 shallot, finely chopped
50ml cider vinegar
sea salt and freshly ground
    black pepper

For the rillettes
4 confit duck legs (see page 120)
200g duck fat
1–2 teaspoons sea salt, to taste

To serve
crusty French bread

To make the chutney, place the sugar in a small heavy-based saucepan over medium heat and cook until the sugar dissolves, swirling the pan occasionally. Bring to the boil and keep cooking until you have a golden brown caramel, about 3 minutes. Immediately stir in the figs, sultanas, peaches and shallot (be careful as it may spit) and cook for about 2–3 minutes. Add the vinegar, stirring to deglaze the pan, and cook for a further 3 minutes. Remove from the heat and leave to cool, then season with salt and pepper to taste.

To make the rillettes, strip the skin and flesh from the duck legs (discard the bones) and place in a food processor, along with the duck fat and salt. Blitz to a coarse consistency. Transfer the rillettes to a dish and serve with the chutney and some crusty bread.

Simple, bold flavours are the secret of this dish, and the flavours you could add are endless: try mushrooms, salmon, chicken – or ham, as here.

BAKED EGGS
WITH BAYONNE HAM & PARSLEY CREAM

SERVES FOUR

40g butter, softened
4–8 slices Bayonne ham
8 eggs
2 tablespoons chopped
  flat-leaf parsley
100ml double cream
sea salt and freshly ground
  black pepper
crusty French bread, to serve

Preheat the oven to 150°C/300°F/gas mark 2.

Generously butter 4 individual ovenproof dishes or ramekins and place on a baking tray. Divide the ham slices between the dishes, laying them over the base and up the sides. Crack 2 eggs into each dish and then top with some of the parsley and the cream. Season with salt and pepper and bake for 12–15 minutes until the eggs are just set.

Scatter over a little more parsley and serve warm, with crusty French bread.

Omelettes are a staple for late suppers at French cafés, hotels and B&Bs. Without an evening omelette menu, I reckon most of the filming crew would have starved!

SMOKED SALMON & CHEDDAR OMELETTE
WITH WATERCRESS

SERVES ONE

15g butter
3 eggs, whisked
50g smoked salmon,
  cut into strips
50g Cheddar cheese, grated
small bunch of watercress
freshly ground black pepper

Heat the grill to high.

Melt the butter in a small non-stick frying pan over low heat until foaming, then add the eggs. Using a spatula, fold the edges in on themselves and cook for 1– 2 minutes until the omelette is almost set. Remove from the heat.

Arrange the salmon over the top of the omelette. Sprinkle with the cheese, then place the omelette under the grill for 1–2 minutes until lightly browned and set.

Season with black pepper, scoop onto a plate and garnish with watercress.

This spur-of-the-moment creation is a riff on a summertime theme, with fresh seafood and ripe melon – and gin and tonic, of course. Not really a classic combination but hey, what the hell... I just enjoyed cooking it.

GIN & TONIC BATTERED ONION RINGS
WITH PRAWN & MELON SALAD

SERVES TWO

For the salad
1 ripe galia melon
25ml raspberry vinegar
75ml grapeseed oil, plus
    1 tablespoon extra
10 tarragon leaves
100g cooked and peeled crayfish
12 cooked and peeled prawns
2 ripe peaches, stones removed
    and flesh diced

For the onion rings
vegetable oil, for deep-frying
200g plain flour
75ml gin
50ml tonic water
2 large white onions,
    thickly sliced into rings

Start by making the salad. Cut the melon in half and discard the seeds. Using a melon baller (sometimes called a Parisienne scoop), scoop the melon into balls and set aside. Over a large bowl, squeeze the melon halves so any remaining juices are reserved in the bowl. Add the raspberry vinegar, grapeseed oil and tarragon leaves, then stir well and set aside to infuse.

Place a non-stick frying pan over medium heat, drizzle in the extra tablespoon of oil and add the melon balls. Fry quickly for 1 minute, shaking the pan, then add the crayfish and prawns and cook for about 30 seconds, just to warm them through. Remove from the heat and add to the bowl with the dressing. Finally, add the peaches to the salad and gently toss everything together.

For the onion rings, heat the vegetable oil in a deep-fat fryer to 180°C/350°F or in a deep heavy-based saucepan until a breadcrumb sizzles and turns brown when dropped into it (note: hot oil can be dangerous; do not leave unattended).

Sift the flour into a clean bowl, then pour in the gin followed by the tonic water, stir well. Working in batches, dip the onion rings into the batter and then deep-fry in the hot oil for 3–4 minutes until crisp and golden brown. Drain on kitchen paper.

To serve, arrange the salad on a platter and top with the onion rings.

I love cooking with brioche, not just in desserts but in dishes such as this, where the sweet buttery nature of brioche brings out the flavour of the pumpkin. If you prefer a less sweet result, try making it with croissants instead of brioche, and with leeks in place of the pumpkin. Served with a crisp green salad, this makes a perfect light lunch.

PUMPKIN, GRUYÈRE & BRIOCHE BAKE

1kg pumpkin, peeled
  and diced
50ml olive oil
6 eggs
400ml double cream
100g Gruyère cheese,
  grated
200g brioche, cubed
sea salt and freshly
  ground black pepper

Preheat the oven to 200°C/400°F/gas mark 6.

Place the pumpkin on a baking tray, drizzle with the olive oil and season with salt and pepper. Roast the pumpkin for 20 minutes or until tender and golden brown.

Meanwhile, in a bowl, whisk the eggs and cream together with a fork, then stir in half the cheese.

Transfer the pumpkin to a large ovenproof dish. Pour in the egg mixture and top with the brioche and remaining cheese. Season with salt and pepper, then bake for 20 minutes until puffed up and golden.

Love them or hate them, when cooked well, with golden chanterelle mushrooms, a touch of cream and a little brandy, chicken livers can be a revelation. I cooked this at the same Burgundy vineyard Floyd visited back in 1986, Domaine René Leclerc. I remember setting the tea towels on fire, just as he would have done – and drinking a bottle of red wine, just as he would have done.

WARM CHICKEN LIVERS
& CHANTERELLES ON TOAST

SERVES FOUR

25g butter
25ml olive oil
400g chicken livers, trimmed
400g chanterelle mushrooms
1 shallot, finely diced
2 garlic cloves, crushed
50ml brandy
1 tablespoon Dijon mustard
75ml double cream
½ teaspoon cayenne pepper
4 slices of ciabatta, toasted
sea salt and freshly ground
   black pepper

Heat the butter and oil in a large frying pan over high heat. When it is hot, add the chicken livers, chanterelles, shallot and garlic and cook for 3–4 minutes, stirring occasionally, until the livers and mushrooms are browned.

Add the brandy and bring to the boil, then stir in the mustard, cream and cayenne pepper and season to taste with salt and pepper.

Spoon the chicken livers, chanterelles and sauce onto the toast and serve immediately.

The ultimate cheese and ham toastie... Simple. I love it.

CROQUE MONSIEUR

8 thick slices white bread
100g Cheddar cheese, grated
4 thick slices ham
100g butter
sea salt and freshly ground
  black pepper

For the béchamel sauce
25g butter
25g plain flour
300ml milk

For the béchamel sauce, melt the butter in a small saucepan over low heat. Stir in the flour using a wooden spoon, then cook gently for 1 minute, still stirring. Remove the pan from the heat and gradually whisk in the milk until smooth. Return the pan to the heat and continue to cook, stirring constantly with the wooden spoon, until the sauce thickens. Season with salt and pepper, then remove from the heat and leave until cold.

To make the sandwiches, spread a layer of the béchamel sauce over one side of four slices of the bread, then top each one with cheese, ham and another slice of bread.

Melt the butter in a large, non-stick frying pan until foaming, fry the sandwiches, two at a time, for 2–3 minutes on each side. Serve with a sprinkle of sea salt.

FISH

Sounds glam – and, I've got to be honest, it is – but a splash of Champagne in sauces for fish dishes works a treat. To open the scallops, ease a small sharp knife between the two halves of the shell and wiggle to prise open, or ask your fishmonger to do this for you.

SCALLOPS SAINT JACQUES
WITH CHAMPAGNE SAUCE

SERVES FOUR

For the scallops
300g baking potatoes, washed
12 scallops in the shell
about 300g cooking salt
2 egg yolks
125g butter
1 banana shallot, finely chopped
1 carrot, finely diced
4 baby leeks, trimmed
  and finely chopped
2 sticks celery, finely chopped
15g Gruyère cheese, finely grated
15g fine breadcrumbs
sea salt and freshly ground
  black pepper

For the sauce
110g butter
2 shallots, finely sliced
150ml white wine
150ml fish stock
150ml double cream
110ml Champagne
2 tomatoes, skinned
  (see page 14), deseeded
  and finely diced
1 tablespoon finely
  chopped chervil
1 tablespoon finely
  chopped tarragon
1 tablespoon finely
  chopped chives
½ lemon, juiced

Preheat the oven to 220°C/425°F/gas mark 7. Prick the potatoes all over with the tip of a knife then bake in the oven for 45 minutes or until cooked through.

Meanwhile, remove the scallops from the shells, clean well and trim away any grey muscle, leaving the main flesh of the scallop. Scrub four of the deep halves of the shells clean, rinse well then place in the oven for a couple of minutes to dry out. Make four mounds of cooking salt on a baking tray and nestle a scallop shell on each one so they sit flat.

Leave the baked potatoes to cool for a few minutes before cutting them in half and scooping out the flesh. Pass the potato flesh through a ricer into a bowl (or finely mash with a potato masher), then add the egg yolks and 25g of the butter and work with a wooden spatula until smooth. Season lightly with salt and pepper, then transfer to a piping bag fitted with a star nozzle and set aside.

Season the scallops with salt and pepper. Heat a frying pan until hot, add 50g of the butter and cook the scallops for 1–1½ minutes each side until golden brown. Remove from the pan and drain on kitchen paper.

Heat a large sauté pan over low to medium heat, add the remaining 50g butter and fry the shallot, carrot, leeks and celery for 10 minutes until soft. Divide these between the scallop shells, then place three scallops in each shell on top of the vegetables.

To make the sauce, heat a frying pan until hot, add the butter and shallots and fry over low heat for 2–3 minutes. Add the white wine and reduce by half, then add the fish stock and reduce that by half. Add the cream and reduce by half and then finally add the Champagne, tomatoes, herbs and lemon juice. Season with salt and pepper to taste.

Heat the grill to high. Pour the Champagne sauce over the scallops, then pipe the potato mixture around the edge of each scallop shell. Sprinkle with the Gruyère cheese and breadcrumbs. Place the baking tray under the grill for 1–2 minutes until the sauce is lightly glazed and the potato border is pale golden.

BBQ MIXED SEAFOOD
IN A BAG ON A BOAT

SERVES TWO

¼ large fennel bulb, trimmed
1 leek, trimmed
2 large spring onions, trimmed
100g samphire
300g mussels, cleaned
  (see page 52)
300g clams, cleaned
6 small scallops
8 raw tiger prawns, shell on
2 large raw langoustines, shell on
2 large pinches of chopped
  flat-leaf parsley
2 large pinches of chopped
  chervil
200ml dry white wine

Preheat the BBQ: when the coals are silvery in colour, it's ready. Alternatively, preheat the oven to 180°C/350°F/gas mark 4.

To make the parcels, tear off two pieces of foil about 60cm long, then two pieces of greaseproof paper about 30cm long. Place one piece of foil on a clean flat surface, shiny side down. Make a fold line down the centre of one sheet of the greaseproof paper, open it flat and place on top of the foil so it looks like the open page of a book. Do the same with the other pieces of foil and greaseproof paper.

Thinly slice the fennel. Cut the leek and spring onions in half lengthways and then into thin strips. Place half of the fennel on one side of the greaseproof paper, then top with half of the samphire. Next come half of the mussels and clams, followed by three scallops, four prawns and one langoustine. Place half the strips of leek and spring onion on top, then scatter over half of the herbs. Season well with salt and pepper. Repeat for the second parcel.

Now fold the greaseproof and foil over the top of the seafood mixture and crimp together the edges to seal the parcels, leaving a little opening in the middle of each one – it should look like a giant Cornish pasty. Carefully pour half the wine in through the opening, then the parcel closed. Repeat the process for the second parcel.

Place the parcels, seam side up, on the BBQ or in the oven and cook for 8 minutes. Remove and allow to stand for 2–3 minutes before serving.

A classic French dish I just had to include in the book, plus I waited ages at a market stall in Marseille to buy this piece of fish, and it didn't disappoint.

PAN-FRIED SKATE WING
WITH NUT-BROWN BUTTER

SERVES TWO

25ml olive oil
300g skate wing, trimmed
125g butter
1 shallot, finely chopped
75g baby capers, rinsed
  and drained
2 lemons, juiced
small bunch of flat-leaf
  parsley, leaves picked
  and roughly chopped
sea salt and freshly
  ground black pepper

Place a heavy-based non-stick frying pan over medium heat, then drizzle in the olive oil. When the oil is hot, add the skate wing to the pan and allow to cook for 3–4 minutes until golden brown. Using a fish slice, turn the skate over and cook on the other side for another 3–4 minutes until just cooked. Remove the skate from the pan and place on a warm serving platter.

Add the butter to the same pan and let it turn a nut-brown colour before adding the shallot. Reduce the heat and cook gently for 1 minute, then add the capers and lemon juice and cook for about 2 minutes before adding the parsley. Season with salt and pepper.

Pour the caper and lemon nut-brown butter over the skate wing and serve at once.

MOULES MARINIÈRE

SERVES TWO

1kg live mussels
2 tablespoons olive oil
1 onion, finely chopped
2 garlic cloves, finely chopped
150ml white wine
2 sprigs of thyme
150ml double cream
small bunch of flat-leaf parsley,
   leaves picked and chopped
crusty bread, to serve

Rinse the mussels thoroughly under plenty of running water and pull off the stringy beards, throwing away any broken shells and any that don't close tightly when you tap them.

Take a large heavy-based pan with a snug-fitting lid and heat the olive oil. Add the onion and garlic and cook over low heat for about 5 minutes until soft. Pour in the wine and as it boils and the alcohol burns off, add the mussels and thyme. Cover and let the mussels steam for 3–4 minutes. They are ready when the shells have opened. Add the cream and cook for 1 minute more.

Scatter with parsley and serve immediately with crusty bread, remembering to discard any mussels that haven't opened.

You wouldn't normally associate tinned food with French cuisine, but they use tinned meat, fish, vegetables, beans and pulses in creative ways, from confit to cassoulet – and it's bloody lovely. Here, a tin of beans pepped up with chorizo makes the perfect foil for some seared scallops.

PAN-FRIED SCALLOPS
WITH WHITE BEANS & CHORIZO

SERVES TWO

50g butter
8 scallops, cleaned, with any
   grey muscle trimmed away
100g spicy chorizo, cut into
   5mm slices
1 shallot, finely chopped
2 garlic cloves, finely chopped
2 plum tomatoes, cut into chunks
1 x 200g jar of cooked haricot
   beans (or 200g tinned haricot
   beans), drained and rinsed
75ml white wine
squeeze of lemon juice
10 basil leaves
sea salt and freshly ground
   black pepper

Place a high-sided frying pan (or a non-stick saucepan) over medium heat and add the butter. When it is hot, add the scallops and sear for 1 minute each side, then remove with a slotted spoon and set aside.

Add the chorizo to the pan and fry for 2–3 minutes. Add the shallot and garlic and cook for 2 more minutes. Add the tomatoes, beans and white wine and bring to the boil. Cover with a lid and cook for a further 5 minutes.

Remove the lid, return the scallops to the pan and warm through for 30 seconds. Add a squeeze of lemon juice, season with salt and pepper, and serve topped with the basil leaves.

*I cooked this on a horse ranch in the Camargue with a load of cowboys,
like you do, for no reason other than I really needed a BBQ to get rid of all
the flies on a seriously hot and humid day. Happily, this light and spicy
dish is just the thing to eat in warmer weather.*

BBQ RED MULLET
WITH PUMPKIN PICKLE

SERVES TWO

2 whole red mullet,
  scaled and gutted
2 limes, 1 thinly sliced,
  1 cut in half
¼ red onion, thinly sliced
2 garlic cloves, thinly sliced
10 mint leaves
25g unsalted butter
sea salt and freshly ground
  black pepper

For the pumpkin pickle
500g pumpkin, peeled and diced
25g unsalted butter, softened
¼ red onion, thinly sliced
2 garlic cloves, thinly sliced
100g mango chutney
1 tablespoon curry powder
½ teaspoon turmeric
½ teaspoon ground coriander
1 lime, juiced
1 star anise
10 mint leaves, chopped
1 tablespoon chopped parsley

Preheat the BBQ: when the coals are silvery in colour, it's ready.

Meanwhile, make the pickle. Cook the pumpkin in a saucepan of
salted boiling water for 10–15 minutes until tender, then drain and set
aside. Place a high-sided frying pan over medium heat, add the butter
and fry the onion and garlic for 2 minutes, then add the pumpkin and
he mango chutney. Mix all the ground spices with a tablespoon of water
in a small bowl, then add to the pan and cook for a further 5 minutes.
Add the lime juice, stir well and season with salt and pepper, then
remove from the heat.

To prepare the fish, lay them flat on a clean board and tuck the lime
slices, onion, garlic and mint leaves into their cavities. Season with
salt and pepper.

Rub each fish with half the butter and cook on the BBQ (or a hot
chargrill pan) for 4–5 minutes. Place the lime halves, cut side down,
on the BBQ next to the fish and allow to char. At the same time turn
the fish over and cook for a further 4–5 minutes.

To finish the pumpkin pickle, add the star anise, mint and parsley,
stir well and cook gently for 3 minutes. Spoon the pickle onto serving
plates and serve with the mullet and the charred limes.

LOBSTER TAGLIATELLE
WITH CHERRY TOMATOES & BASIL ON A LAKE

SERVES FOUR TO SIX

2 cooked lobsters, meat
  removed from shells
1 tablespoon olive oil
3 garlic cloves, thinly sliced
1 small red chilli, diced
400g cherry tomatoes,
  left whole
3 sprigs of tarragon,
  leaves picked
100ml double cream
25ml brandy
400g fresh tagliatelle
small bunch of basil,
  leaves picked
50g freshly grated Parmesan
sea salt and freshly ground
  black pepper

In a large non-stick frying pan, heat the oil and gently fry the garlic and chilli over low heat for 3–4 minutes until softened. Add the tomatoes and tarragon and cook for 2 minutes until the tomatoes start to soften. Pour in the cream and brandy and simmer gently for 10 minutes until the sauce has thickened slightly.

Meanwhile, bring a large saucepan of water to the boil, add a teaspoon of salt and cook the tagliatelle for 2–3 minutes. Drain the pasta and return to the pan, reserving 50ml of the pasta cooking water.

Gently stir the lobster meat into the tomato sauce and warm through. Carefully tip the lobster and all the sauce into the tagliatelle, along with the reserved cooking water, and stir to combine. Transfer to a large warmed platter and top with the basil leaves and Parmesan.

Also known as Saint Peter's fish, after the patron saint of fishermen, John Dory is a beautiful fish. This was the first dish I cooked on the show, and no sooner had I finished and walked away to wash my hands than some eager French people huddled around the pan and started to dive in. A vote of confidence, if ever I saw one!

WHOLE JOHN DORY
WITH CLAMS & COURGETTES

SERVES TWO

2 courgettes, thickly sliced
2 heritage tomatoes,
  thickly sliced
2 shallots, thinly sliced
1 x 1kg John Dory, gutted
  and fins removed
50ml olive oil
375ml dry white wine
15 basil leaves
300g clams, washed
handful of flat-leaf
  parsley leaves
sea salt and freshly
  ground black pepper

Preheat the oven to 200°C/400°F/gas mark 6.

Arrange the courgettes and tomatoes over the base of a roasting tin. Slot the shallot slices in between the courgettes and tomatoes. Season with salt and pepper.

Season the John Dory with salt and pepper, place on top of the vegetables and drizzle with half the olive oil. Pour the white wine over and scatter with the basil leaves. Cover tightly with foil and cook in the oven for 20 minutes. Carefully lift off the foil and add the clams, then cover again and return to the oven for a further 5 minutes or until the clams open up (discard any that remain closed).

Remove from the oven, scatter over the parsley leaves and add a final drizzle of olive oil.

Red mullet are little used in the UK, but when you can get your hands on some, simple is the way to go. This warm olive oil and lemon juice dressing is a good place to start, or stick with tradition and cook the fish whole, then spread their liver on small toasts – a highly prized delicacy in France.

RED MULLET
WITH SAUCE VIERGE

SERVES TWO

300ml olive oil
2 red mullet, filleted
½ red onion, finely diced
1 garlic clove, finely chopped
3 tomatoes, deseeded and diced
1 teaspoon coriander seeds,
   crushed
small bunch each of parsley,
   chervil, dill and basil, chopped
2 lemons, juiced
sea salt and freshly ground
   black pepper, to taste

Heat a large non-stick frying pan over medium heat, add 1 tablespoon of the oil and fry the mullet fillets, skin side down, for 2 minutes. Flip them over and immediately take the pan off the heat, but leave the fish to cook through in the pan.

Meanwhile, gently warm the remaining oil in a small saucepan. Add all the remaining ingredients and heat through for about 30 seconds.

Transfer the fish fillets to warmed plates and spoon over the sauce.

In its shroud of salt, this fish may look odd, but it tastes off the scale! You can do it with whatever fish you please – just make sure you use good-quality sea salt. As I bought my sea bass from the market in Marseille, straight off the boat, I just had to use the Camargue salt that's so famous in southern France.

SALT-BAKED SEA BASS

SERVES FOUR TO SIX

1 x 2kg sea bass, scaled,
  gutted and head removed
2 lemons, 1 thinly sliced,
  1 cut into wedges
small bunch of dill, chopped
  (retain the stalks)
6 egg whites
1kg sea salt
1 tablespoon pink peppercorns,
  lightly crushed
2 teaspoons dried herbes
  de Provence
lemon wedges, to serve

Preheat the oven to 180°C/350°F/gas mark 4. Rinse and dry the sea bass and lay it flat on a board. Pop the slices of lemon and dill stalks in the cavity of the fish.

Place the egg whites in a large, clean, dry bowl and whisk until nearly at soft-peak stage, then gently fold in the salt, chopped dill, pink peppercorns and herbes de Provence.

Spread a third of the egg white mixture onto a baking tray, keeping it roughly the same shape, but a little larger than, the fish. Place the fish on top, then spread the remaining egg white mixture all over the fish so it is totally covered. Bake in the oven for 30–40 minutes.

Remove the fish from the oven and leave to cool slightly before cracking and discarding the crust. Peel back the skin of the sea bass and lift the flesh from the fish, leaving the bones behind. Place on serving plates and serve with lemon wedges.

I had to do this, if only to wind up the production team. We were in La Bresse at the time, a region famous for its chicken, visiting the chicken museum there. However, after seeing their formidable collection of egg cups and a lot of chicken, I noticed green beans growing in their garden and thought I'd do trout. Tenuous link, I know, but this is so simple and so delicious: brown butter with lean trout, crunchy almonds and fresh green beans.

WHOLE TROUT
WITH ALMONDS & GREEN BEANS

SERVES TWO

2 whole trout, gutted and cleaned
1 tablespoon each chopped
   chervil, chives, parsley and dill
150g green beans, trimmed
150g butter
1 lemon, juiced
50g flaked almonds, toasted
sea salt and freshly ground
   black pepper

Season the trout inside and out and place half the chopped herbs inside the cavities. Place the trout, side by side, on a trivet and place in a large saucepan or high-sided frying pan. Pour in enough water to cover the bottom of the pan to a depth of about 1cm, making sure the water's not touching the fish. Cover the pan with a tight-fitting lid and steam over medium heat for 5 minutes.

Meanwhile, blanch the green beans in a saucepan of simmering water for 3 minutes. Drain and set aside.

Melt the butter in a small saucepan and cook over medium heat until nut-brown and foaming. Add the lemon juice, beans and almonds and cook for a minute, then sprinkle over the remaining herbs.

Remove the skin from the trout, put them on a platter and pour over the green bean mixture.

I used two different sorts of clams for this but you can use just one, or even mussels if you want. Thankfully, samphire is now increasingly available, but is best bought fresh rather than pickled.

CLAMS IN FENNEL & CHIVE SAUCE
WITH SAMPHIRE

SERVES FOUR

12 razor clams, cleaned
500g clams, cleaned
150ml white wine
2 tablespoons olive oil
1 garlic clove, finely chopped
2 shallots, finely chopped
1 fennel bulb, trimmed
   and finely diced
150ml double cream
1 teaspoon finely chopped
   chives
2 plum tomatoes, skinned
   (see page 14), deseeded
   and diced
200g samphire

Heat a large saucepan until hot, add all the clams and the wine, cover with a lid and steam over high heat for 1–2 minutes or until the clams have opened. Pour the contents of the pan into a colander set over a bowl and drain. Keep the liquor.

Discard any clams that haven't opened, then pull the clams from the shells and remove the dark grey part from the razor clams. Reserve half the razor clam shells and discard most of the round shells. Rinse the clams to remove any grit, then roughly chop the flesh.

Place a sauté pan over medium heat, add the oil and heat until hot. Add the garlic and shallots and cook for 2–3 minutes, stirring, until soft. Add the fennel and cook for a further 2–3 minutes until tender. Add the clam liquor and cream and cook until reduced by half, about 5 minutes.

To finish, add the clam flesh, chives, tomatoes and samphire and gently warm through for 30 seconds. Arrange the reserved shells on a large warmed platter and spoon the clams and sauce over the shells to serve.

Beurre blanc was one of the first sauces I learnt to make when I started my training in France as a teenager. So when I had the idea for this TV series, this was among the first dishes I wanted to cook.

STEAMED LING
WITH TURNED VEGETABLES & BEURRE BLANC

SERVES TWO

2 x 175g portions ling
  or hake
25g butter, in small knobs
100g baby spinach
  leaves, washed
drizzle of olive oil

For the turned vegetables
1 green courgette
1 yellow courgette
1 carrot

For the beurre blanc
50ml white wine vinegar
40ml white wine
1 banana shallot,
  roughly chopped
6 white peppercorns
1 bay leaf
sprig of thyme
200g chilled unsalted
  butter, diced
small bunch of chives,
  finely chopped
sea salt and freshly
  ground black pepper

If you are using ling, season with salt and leave it to sit at room temperature while you prepare the vegetables and sauce.

For the turned vegetables, cut the courgettes and carrot crossways into 4, giving you 12 pieces of vegetable. Now, for the tricky bit: hold each vegetable piece between your index finger and thumb, and take a small paring knife in your other hand. Place the knife at the top of the vegetable and pull it towards you to give the vegetable a smooth curved shape – be careful not to cut your thumb. Repeat this around all sides of the vegetable until it looks like a mini-barrel, then do the same for the other vegetables. Set aside.

For the beurre blanc, place the white wine vinegar, white wine, shallots, peppercorns, bay leaf and thyme in a saucepan. Bring to a rapid boil and then turn down to a simmer and cook until reduced by two-thirds. Turn the heat down to very low and slowly whisk in the cold butter a little at a time, whisking well between each addition. Remove from the heat and pass the sauce through a fine sieve. Discard what is left in the sieve and keep the sauce in a warm (but not hot) place.

Pour a 2cm depth of water into the bottom of a steamer pan or saucepan, top with the steamer basket and place over low to medium heat. When the water is simmering, add the vegetables to the steamer basket and cook for 3–4 minutes. Cut a piece of greaseproof paper large enough to hold the 2 pieces of fish. Lay the fish on the greaseproof paper and then place on top of the vegetables. Cover and cook for 5 minutes.

Remove the steamer basket with the fish and vegetables in it and set aside. Drain the water from the pan, then add the knobs of butter, drop in the spinach and let it wilt for a minute. Divide the spinach between serving plates and top with the fish fillets. Add the other vegetables to the pan and gently toss in the butter. Arrange the buttery vegetables around the spinach in alternating colours. Stir the chopped chives into the beurre blanc, then spoon over the fish.

Sometimes the simplest things are the best: tender morsels of fish in a crunchy coating with a sharp tartare sauce. Just perfect accompanied by a green leaf salad dressed with olive oil and lemon juice.

SOLE GOUJONS
WITH TARTARE SAUCE

SERVES TWO

450g Dover sole or lemon
   sole fillets, skinned
125g fresh fine breadcrumbs
½ teaspoon cayenne pepper
sunflower oil, for deep-frying
50g plain flour
3 eggs, beaten
sea salt and freshly ground
   black pepper
lemon wedges, to serve

For the tartare sauce
100g mayonnaise
2 tablespoons chopped capers
4 chopped gherkins
1 tablespoon chopped
   flat-leaf parsley

To make the tartare sauce, combine all the ingredients in a small bowl and season. Set aside.

For the goujons, heat the oil in a deep-fat fryer to 190°C/375°F or in a deep heavy-based saucepan until a breadcrumb sizzles and turns brown when dropped into it (note: hot oil can be dangerous; do not leave unattended).

Cut the sole fillets on the diagonal into strips about 2cm thick. Mix the breadcrumbs with the cayenne pepper on a plate, put the flour on a separate plate and the beaten eggs in a bowl.

Working in batches, coat a few of the fish strips in flour, then the beaten egg and finally the breadcrumbs. Carefully place into the hot oil and cook for about 1 minute until crisp and golden brown, then drain on kitchen paper. Repeat until all the goujons are cooked.

Pile the goujons in a dish or on plates and serve with lemon wedges and tartare sauce.

Wreck fish is a firm white-fleshed fish similar to grey mullet or sea bass, either of which can be used here, as can hake, cod or haddock. What I love about this dish is the buckwheat – it's something we don't use often enough, and the brown butter makes the most of its nutty, peppery taste.

WRECK FISH & CRAYFISH
WITH BEURRE NOISETTE BUCKWHEAT

SERVES TWO

24 raw crayfish tails
50g butter
2 wreck fish or sea bass
   fillets, skin on, pin boned
100g samphire

For the bisque
1 tablespoon olive oil
50g butter
2 shallots, finely chopped
1 fennel bulb, trimmed
   and finely chopped
1 tablespoon tomato purée
500g crayfish shells (see above)
2 tablespoons brandy
1 litre fish stock
2 bay leaves
2 sprigs of flat-leaf parsley
sea salt and freshly ground
   black pepper

For the buckwheat
100g buckwheat
50g unsalted butter

Start by blanching the crayfish tails. Bring a large saucepan of water to the boil, add the crayfish tails and cook for 1 minute. Immediately drain and refresh under cold water. Carefully pull the meat from the shells, reserving both the shells and the crayfish meat.

To make the bisque, heat the oil and butter in a large frying pan and gently fry the shallots and fennel for 2–3 minutes until softened. Add the tomato purée and cook, stirring, for 1 minute. Add the crayfish shells and brandy and cook for a further minute. Add the fish stock, bay leaves and parsley and bring to a simmer. Cook for 20–25 minutes, or until the volume of liquid has reduced by a third. Remove from the heat and allow to cool slightly, then pour into a food processor and blend to a fine purée. Pass the purée through a sieve into a clean saucepan and season the bisque to taste with salt and pepper. Keep warm.

Cook the buckwheat in a saucepan of simmering salted water for 10–15 minutes until just tender, then drain. Heat a large sauté pan over medium heat and add the butter. Once it has turned brown, add the buckwheat and sauté for 2 minutes until hot and coated in the butter.

Meanwhile, heat a large frying pan and add 25g of the butter. Once hot, add the fish fillets and crayfish meat and cook for 2 minutes on each side. Heat a large sauté pan over medium heat and add the remaining 25g of butter. When it's hot, add the samphire and cook for 1–2 minutes.

To serve, put some buckwheat on serving plates, then place some samphire alongside. Spoon some bisque onto the plate, then top with the wreck fish and crayfish.

This uses the small baby artichokes that need less trimming than the fully grown ones – they're quite seasonal, so grab them when you see them.

LAMB CUTLETS
WITH ARTICHOKES, TOMATOES & OLIVES

SERVES TWO

6 small globe artichokes
50ml olive oil
6 lamb cutlets
2 lemons, 1 halved, 1 juiced
100g whole red and yellow
   baby cherry tomatoes
100g black olives, pitted
15 anchovy fillets, drained
   and chopped
50g flat-leaf parsley, chopped
sea salt and freshly ground
   black pepper

To prepare the artichokes, remove the stalks and all the outer leaves. Scrape out and discard the hairy 'choke' from the middle to leave just the base of the artichokes. Rub the bases with a lemon half and then cut into wedges.

Place a high-sided frying pan over medium heat, drizzle with the olive oil and heat until hot. Season the lamb cutlets with salt and pepper and cook for 2–3 minutes each side for medium (3–4 minutes each side for well done), then remove from the pan and set aside to rest.

Add the artichokes to the same pan used for the lamb and cook over medium heat for 2–3 minutes before adding the tomatoes, olives and anchovies. Cover with a lid and cook for a further 2–3 minutes.

Finally add the parsley, squeeze over the lemon juice and season with salt and pepper. Mix well, then spoon the artichoke mixture onto serving plates, top with the lamb cutlets and serve.

A couple of tips for you: use meaty Toulouse sausages for this, and whenever you're cooking Puy lentils, a touch of sherry vinegar works a treat. I ate this for lunch in Saint-Émilion with a lovely a bottle of quite expensive red wine... With a budget to stick to, I chose the cheapest dish on the menu and the best bottle of plonk!

SAUSAGES
WITH PUY LENTILS

SERVES FOUR

2 tablespoons rapeseed oil
100g pancetta, diced
2 shallots, finely chopped
1 garlic clove, finely chopped
1 small carrot, finely chopped
1 stick celery, finely chopped
1 leek, finely chopped
300g Puy lentils
175ml red wine
450ml veal jus or stock
8 Toulouse sausages
25ml olive oil
2 tablespoons sherry vinegar
2 tablespoons chopped parsley

Place a sauté pan over medium heat and add the rapeseed oil. When hot, add the pancetta and cook for 2–3 minutes until golden. Add the shallot and cook for 2–3 minutes, then add the garlic, carrot, celery and leek and cook for a further 2 minutes until softened. Add the lentils and red wine and bring to the boil. Cook until the wine has reduced by half, then add the stock and turn the heat down to a simmer. Cook for 20–30 minutes until the lentils are tender.

Meanwhile, heat a large frying pan over low to medium heat and gently fry the sausages in the olive oil until they are golden brown and cooked through.

To serve, stir the sherry vinegar and parsley through the lentils, then pile the lentils into bowls and top with the sausages.

*When I found these amazing carrots (pictured over the page) at the market,
I just knew I had to make this dish. Alongside some top-quality pork from
the same market, this is the way we should all cook. Interestingly, in every
Michelin-starred restaurant we went to on the trip they served carrots,
carrots with everything. And when you've got carrots this good, why not?*

PORK WITH VICHY CARROTS

SERVES FOUR

For the Vichy carrots
150g caster sugar
250g butter
5 star anise
16 carrots, with tops on

For the pork
4 pork loin chops
    (about 1.5kg in total)
2 tablespoons olive oil
sea salt and freshly
    ground black pepper

For the carrots, pour 1 litre of water into a large shallow pan, add
the sugar, butter and star anise and bring to the boil. Peel the carrots
and cut off the tops, leaving 5cm of green still attached. Finely chop
2 tablespoons of the carrot tops and reserve. Add the carrots to the
pan and boil rapidly for 20 minutes until tender.

Meanwhile, season the chops with pepper only. Place a large non-
stick frying pan over high heat and pour in the oil. When it is hot, add
the chops and cook for 6–8 minutes, turning half way through, until
browned and cooked through. Remove from the heat, season with
salt and leave to rest for 5 minutes.

To finish the carrots, stir the finely chopped carrot tops into the
reduced cooking liquid in the pan and serve up. Place four carrots
on each plate, top with a chop, then spoon over the sauce.

There are so many variations of classic pepper sauce, and this is mine. The inspiration for it came from a fantastic restaurant in Lyon, where they served splendidly rich food, but you can loosen it up with a touch more cream if you wish.

STEAK AU POIVRE
WITH WILTED SPINACH

SERVES FOUR

4 x 200g rib-eye steaks
3 tablespoons cracked black
   peppercorns
100g butter
75ml red wine
100ml beef stock
3 tablespoons green peppercorns,
   in brine, drained
100ml double cream
200g baby leaf spinach, washed
2 garlic cloves, peeled but
   left whole
pinch of freshly grated nutmeg
sea salt and freshly ground
   black pepper

Season the steaks with a little salt and the cracked black peppercorns pressing the peppercorns well into the meat, shaking off any excess.

Heat a frying pan until hot and add 75g of the butter, then add the steaks two at a time (unless you have a very large frying pan) and cook for 2–3 minutes on each side, depending on how you like your steak cooked (about 3–4 minutes each side for medium, or 4–5 minutes for well done). Remove the steaks from the pan and leave in a warm place to rest while you finish the sauce.

Add the red wine to the pan, gently shaking the pan to ignite and cook off the alcohol.

Scrape the bottom of the pan and simmer until the liquid has reduced by half. Add the beef stock and green peppercorns, bring to a simmer and cook for 2 minutes. Add the cream and simmer for a further minute.

Meanwhile, cook the spinach. Heat a frying pan until hot and add the remaining 25g butter. When melted, add the spinach and the garlic cloves. Stir for 1–2 minutes until all the spinach is wilted. Season with nutmeg, salt and pepper. Discard the garlic cloves.

To serve, spoon the spinach onto the plates, place a steak on top and pour over the sauce.

A great piece of meat needs a great sauce, and I rediscovered this one in the Normandy region of France. It was something I hadn't cooked for 15 years, but it was so good it's now on my restaurant menu.

RIB-EYE STEAK
WITH MUSHROOM SAUCE & FRITES

SERVES TWO

For the sauce
750ml chicken stock
2 shallots, thinly sliced
1 garlic clove, finely chopped
50g butter, diced
150g button mushrooms, sliced
100ml white wine
small bunch of tarragon,
  leaves picked

For the steaks
2 x 250g rib-eye steaks
1 tablespoon olive oil
50g unsalted butter
sea salt and freshly ground
  black pepper

For the frites
vegetable oil, for deep-frying
4 large baking potatoes, peeled
  and cut into matchsticks
sea salt

To make the sauce, place the stock in a saucepan over medium heat and reduce it until there is about 250ml left. In a frying pan, sauté the shallots and garlic in a knob of the butter over medium heat until golden. Add the mushrooms, then quickly add the wine, half of the tarragon and the reduced stock. Simmer until reduced by half again and thickened, then remove from the heat and whisk in the remaining butter. Add the rest of the tarragon, season and keep warm.

Place a frying pan over high heat. Rub the steaks with the olive oil, place them in the hot pan and allow to cook for 6 minutes before turning over. Add the butter and continue to cook, spooning the butter over the steaks, for a further 6 minutes. (If you like your steak well done, cook for another minute or so on each side.) Remove the steaks from the pan and leave in a warm place to rest for about 5 minutes.

Meanwhile, for the frites, heat the oil in a deep-fat fryer to 190°C/375°F or in a deep heavy-based saucepan until a breadcrumb sizzles and turns brown when dropped into it (note: hot oil can be dangerous; do not leave unattended). Deep-fry the frites in the hot vegetable oil until golden brown, then remove and drain on kitchen paper. Sprinkle with sea salt.

Season the steaks with salt and pepper, then serve with the frites and the sauce on the side.

The city of Lyon is known for its bouchons, rustic restaurants that proudly serve traditional Lyonnaise food. I cooked these pork escalopes at a classic bouchon called Comptoir du Loup Pendu, which had this very dish on its menu. The key to making Lyonnaise potatoes is to par-boil them first, then cook them in plenty of butter.

PORK ESCALOPES
WITH LYONNAISE POTATOES

SERVES TWO TO THREE

For the potatoes
1 large onion, sliced
25ml olive oil
3 large potatoes, peeled and
  par-boiled for 10 minutes,
  then cut into 5mm-thick slices
50g butter
50ml beef stock
small bunch of flat-leaf parsley,
  leaves picked and chopped

For the pork
1 large pork fillet (about 400g),
  cut into 5cm slices
50g plain flour
2 eggs
75g panko breadcrumbs
50g butter
50ml olive oil
sea salt and freshly ground
  black pepper

For the potatoes, fry the onion in the oil in a heavy-based frying pan for a minute or two until softened. Add the potatoes and butter, stir and season with salt and pepper. Cook over medium heat for 10 minutes, stirring occasionally.

For the pork, place the slices between two sheets of cling film and use a rolling pin to flatten them to about 5mm thick. Place the flour in a shallow bowl and season with salt and pepper. Beat the eggs in another bowl, and put the breadcrumbs into a third bowl. Dip each piece of pork in the flour, then in the beaten egg and finally in the breadcrumbs until evenly coated.

In a large non-stick frying pan, heat the butter and oil until bubbling and fry the pork escalopes, two or three at a time, over medium heat for 2 minutes on each side. Remove from the heat and place on a warmed serving platter.

To finish the potatoes, add the stock to the pan, bring to the boil and add the parsley. Serve with the pork.

I was so excited about visiting the Cognac region, and it definitely lived up to expectations. Good Cognac makes for a good sauce – and happy drinking!

FILLET STEAK & DICED POTATOES
WITH PINK PEPPERCORN & COGNAC SAUCE

SERVES TWO

4 medium potatoes
   (about 400g), roughly diced
3 tablespoons olive oil
3 garlic cloves, crushed
2 x 175g fillet steaks
25g unsalted butter
2 shallots, finely diced
25ml Cognac
3 teaspoons pink
   peppercorns, crushed
100ml beef stock
150ml double cream
1 teaspoon Dijon mustard
small bunch of flat-leaf parsley,
   leaves picked and chopped
sea salt and freshly ground
   black pepper

Place a non-stick frying pan over medium heat. When hot, add the potatoes, followed by 2 tablespoons of the olive oil and the garlic. Allow to cook, stirring occasionally, for 15–20 minutes.

Place another non-stick frying pan over high heat. Rub the steaks with the remaining tablespoon of olive oil, then place in the hot pan. Let them cook for 2–3 minutes, then turn them over and continue to cook for a further 2–3 minutes for medium-rare. (Cook the steaks for an extra 2 minutes each side for medium, 4 minutes for well done.)

Add half the butter to the pan and spoon over the top of the steaks for about a minute, then remove the steaks from the pan to a warmed plate and pour over the pan juices. Season with salt and pepper.

Return the steak pan to the heat and add the remaining butter. When it foams, add the shallots and cook over medium heat for 3–4 minutes until golden. Add the Cognac and gently shake the pan – this will ignite the Cognac and burn the alcohol off. When the flame dies down, add the pink peppercorns and continue to cook for about 2 minutes before adding the beef stock. Bring to the boil and then finally add the cream and mustard. Season with salt and pepper, then remove from the heat.

Toss the potatoes, add the parsley and turn the heat off.

Place the steaks on plates, then divide the potatoes between the plates. Spoon the sauce over the steaks and serve.

It's not often that we cook with lettuce, however the French do this so well.
Little gem or cos lettuce are ideal for this fast, simple great-tasting dish.

LAMB CHOPS
WITH SEARED LITTLE GEM & PEAS

SERVES FOUR

4 Barnsley lamb chops
  (about 150g each)
1 tablespoon olive oil
4 little gem lettuce, cut
  into quarters lengthways
250ml beef stock
400g frozen peas
small bunch of mint, leaves
  picked and chopped
25g butter
50ml double cream
sea salt and freshly
  ground black pepper

Heat the grill to high. Season the lamb chops with salt and pepper, then grill for 2–3 minutes each side, or until cooked to your liking. Transfer to a warmed platter and set aside to rest in a warm place.

Meanwhile, place a large frying pan over high heat and drizzle in the oil. Once it's hot, sear the lettuce until charred on all sides. Add the stock, peas and mint and bring to the boil, then turn down to a simmer and reduce the stock by half. Add the butter and reduce by half again, then season with salt and pepper. Finally, stir in the cream and warm through. Serve with the lamb chops.

The French have really embraced different styles of cooking in recent years. Walk around any French supermarket and you will find harissa, ras el hanout and other ingredients for Moroccan and North African food. This fresh, vibrant tabbouleh is a great accompaniment to lamb, but also works well with most meats and fish.

GRIDDLED LAMB CUTLETS
WITH PINE NUT & POMEGRANATE TABBOULEH

SERVES FOUR

For the tabbouleh
175g bulgur wheat
500ml chicken stock, warmed
2 dried chipotle chillies
1 teaspoon caraway seeds
1 teaspoon cumin seeds
1 teaspoon coriander seeds
2 garlic cloves, roughly chopped
2 shallots, roughly chopped
2 red chillies, deseeded and
  roughly chopped
2 tablespoons olive oil
200g pine nuts, toasted
1 pomegranate, seeds removed
small bunch of mint,
  roughly chopped
small bunch of coriander,
  roughly chopped
1 lemon, zested and juiced
sea salt and freshly ground
  black pepper

For the lamb cutlets
8 French-trimmed lamb cutlets
small bunch of rosemary,
  tied with string
50ml olive oil

To make the tabbouleh, place the bulgur wheat in a saucepan, cover with the warm chicken stock, bring to the boil and cook over medium heat for 15–20 minutes until tender. Drain and allow to cool, then tip the bulgur into a large glass bowl.

Meanwhile, soak the dried chillies in hot water for 5 minutes until soft, then drain and place the chillies in a food processor. Heat a small frying pan and warm the caraway, cumin and coriander seeds until they start to give off a strong aroma. Add to the food processor, along with the garlic, shallots, fresh chillies and olive oil. Blend until smooth.

Stir a couple of tablespoons of the spice paste into the bulgur, then stir through the pine nuts, pomegranate seeds, mint, coriander and the lemon zest and juice. Season with salt and pepper.

For the lamb cutlets, heat a large griddle pan over high heat. Dip the rosemary bundle in olive oil and brush the cutlets with the rosemary. Cook the chops for 2 minutes each side for rare, continuing to brush them with the rosemary and oil. (For medium, cook them for an extra minute each side, and for well done, an extra 2 minutes.)

Serve the lamb cutlets with the tabbouleh.

Cooking this on location was a day to remember for many reasons. There was the view, for a start, then the mayor and all his mates turned up unannounced and so I had to cook it for them, plus the mercury hit 36 degrees – not ideal for firing up a BBQ full of old vine prunings. But, cooked over wood with a hint of treacle on the beef, oh dear, it works well, so, so well. Just remember it's not a dessert – it doesn't need a litre of the stuff over it, just a light brushing!

TREACLE-GLAZED RIB-EYE STEAK
WITH BLUE CHEESE SALAD

For the salad
2 egg yolks
½ tablespoon Dijon mustard
2 tablespoons raspberry vinegar
200ml grapeseed oil
3 tablespoons crème fraîche
120g soft blue cheese
2 heads little gem lettuce
2 handfuls of dandelion
   or rocket leaves
sea salt and freshly ground
   black pepper

For the steaks
1 baguette
100ml grapeseed oil
1 garlic bulb, cut in half
4 x 300g rib-eye steaks
2 tablespoons black treacle
2 sprigs of thyme, leaves picked
a splash of Worcestershire sauce
a dash of Tabasco sauce
4 large spring onions

Preheat the BBQ: when the coals are silvery in colour, it's ready.

To make the dressing for the salad, place the egg yolks, mustard and raspberry vinegar in a bowl and whisk together until combined. Very slowly add the grapeseed oil, whisking constantly until you have a smooth mayonnaise-like texture. Add the crème fraîche and crumble in the blue cheese. Whisk again until smooth, then season with salt and pepper and set aside.

For the steaks, slice the baguette lengthways, then cut in half crossways. Drizzle with a little of the oil and char both sides on the BBQ. Remove, then rub the cut surfaces of the garlic over the cut side of the baguette. Roughly chop the baguette and spread out over a large serving platter.

Pour the remaining oil into a bowl, add the black treacle, thyme and Worcestershire and Tabasco sauces, and mix together.

Cook the steaks on the BBQ for 4 minutes, then baste with the treacle mix and cook for 2 more minutes. Carefully turn the steaks, spoon over any remaining treacle and cook for a further 4 minutes. Remove the steaks from the BBQ and leave to rest in a warm place.

Meanwhile, cut the spring onions into four lengthways. Place on the BBQ and cook for 3–4 minutes, turning halfway through.

To serve, tear the little gem and scatter over the chopped baguette, then do the same with the dandelion or rocket leaves and drizzle with some of the dressing. Slice the steaks and arrange over the salad, then drizzle over some more dressing. Top with the spring onions, then add a final drizzle of dressing and serve.

One of the signature ingredients of the Burgundy region of France, mustard makes a lovely simple sauce that's just perfect with these veal escalopes (pictured over the page). The key is to add the mustard at the end, to keep its fresh flavour and taste.

VEAL ESCALOPES IN MUSTARD SAUCE
WITH RATTE POTATOES

SERVES FOUR

For the potatoes
400g ratte or pink fir apple
  potatoes, scrubbed
100g butter
1 garlic bulb, cut in half
sea salt and freshly ground
  black pepper

For the pastry fleurons
1 x 320g ready-made puff
  pastry sheet
1 egg yolk, lightly beaten

For the veal
100g butter
4 x 150g veal escalopes
2 shallots, finely diced
100ml brandy
100ml cream
1 tablespoon Dijon mustard
small bunch of parsley,
  leaves picked and chopped

Par-boil the potatoes in a pan of boiling salted water for 10 minutes, then drain and cut in half lengthways. Melt the butter in a large non-stick frying pan, add the potatoes and garlic, season with salt and pepper and fry over high heat for 10 minutes, shaking the pan occasionally, until browned.

Meanwhile, for the pastry fleurons, preheat the oven to 200°C/400°F/gas mark 6. Line a baking sheet with baking parchment. Lay out the pastry sheet on a work surface and cut out 20 crescent-moon shapes. Transfer to the prepared baking sheet and brush with beaten egg yolk, then bake for 8–10 minutes until golden brown. (This will make more fleurons than you need here, but the rest can be frozen and used to garnish other meat dishes.)

For the veal, melt the butter in another large non-stick frying pan and pan-fry the escalopes over high heat for 2 minutes on each side. Season with salt and pepper, then remove from the pan and leave to rest on a warm plate.

Add the shallots to the same pan and cook over medium heat for 3–4 minutes until softened. Pour in the brandy, gently shaking the pan to flame the brandy, then add the cream and simmer until reduced by half. Stir in the mustard, season with salt and pepper and sprinkle in the parsley. Pop the veal back into the pan and gently warm through.

Place the veal on plates, with the fleurons alongside, and serve the potatoes in a big bowl on the table.

This sauce must be made with good-quality beef stock, as it's the reduction of that and the wine which gives the sauce its flavour – don't even try making it with anything less.

FILLET STEAK
WITH BORDELAISE SAUCE

SERVES FOUR

For the sauce
1–2 tablespoons olive oil
4 banana shallots,
  roughly chopped
375ml good-quality
  red wine
1 bay leaf
4 sprigs of thyme
400ml beef stock
50g unsalted butter

For the steaks
4 x 200g fillet steaks
50g butter
3 tablespoons olive oil
sea salt and freshly
  ground black pepper

For the bordelaise sauce, place a frying pan over medium heat. Add a drizzle of olive oil then the shallots and cook until golden brown. Pour in the red wine and bring to the boil, then drop in the bay leaf and thyme and simmer until reduced by two-thirds. Add the stock, bring back to the boil and again allow to reduce by half.

Meanwhile, for the steaks, place a large frying pan over high heat and season the steaks well with salt and pepper. Add the butter and olive oil to the pan and, when hot and foaming, add the steaks. For medium, cook on one side for 3 minutes, turn and cook for 2 more minutes, then turn off the heat and allow to finish cooking in the pan.

To finish the sauce, stir in the butter and take off the heat. Place the steaks on serving plates, spoon over the sauce and serve.

This dish is the French equivalent of beef stew and dumplings – and, like all beef stews, it needs time to cook to melting tenderness. For an authentic depth of flavour, use good-quality Burgundy, and don't rush things.

BOEUF BOURGUIGNON

SERVES SIX

1kg shin of beef, cut into
  5cm cubes
2 tablespoons plain flour
2 tablespoons olive oil
150g pancetta, cut into
  small chunks
1 shallot, finely chopped
2 onions, sliced
1 garlic clove, crushed
75ml brandy
750ml Burgundy red wine
500ml beef stock
1 bouquet garni – 2 bay leaves,
  2 sprigs of thyme, 2 sprigs
  of flat-leaf parsley, tied
  with string
25g butter
110g baby onions, peeled
  but left whole
200g chestnut mushrooms
sea salt and freshly ground
  black pepper

Toss the beef with the flour and some salt and pepper.

Place a large sauté pan or flameproof casserole over medium heat, add half the olive oil and the pancetta and fry for 1–2 minutes until golden brown. Add the beef and fry until browned on all sides. Add the shallot, onions and garlic and fry until just softened.

Add the brandy and gently shake the pan – this will ignite the brandy and burn the alcohol off. When the flame dies down, pour in the red wine and beef stock and bring to a simmer. Add the bouquet garni, then cover and cook over very low heat for 2 hours or until the beef is tender and the sauce has thickened.

Heat a frying pan until hot, add the butter and the remaining oil and fry the baby onions until just golden. Add to the casserole, along with the chestnut mushrooms, and cook for a further 20 minutes. Check the seasoning before serving.

While we were in Normandy, home of Calvados, we visited the famous Pegasus Bridge, where the liberation of France began on D-Day in 1944. Just a stone's throw away, we found an amazing apple farm in the district of Victot-Pontfol: not only did they produce delicious cider, but they also distilled and aged it to make even more delicious Calvados.

BLACK PUDDING
WITH APPLES & CALVADOS

SERVES SIX

4 Bramley apples,
  peeled and diced
25g butter
50ml Calvados
600g black pudding
sea salt and freshly
  ground black pepper

Heat the grill to high.

Place the apples and butter in a large saucepan with the Calvados and cook gently until the apples are just starting to break down, about 5 minutes. Season with salt and pepper and keep warm.

Cut the black pudding into 1cm-thick slices. Place on a baking tray lined with foil and grill on both sides until crispy.

Serve the black pudding with the apple sauce on the side.

POULTRY & GAME

Not far from the French border with Switzerland, the commune of Copponex is dominated by orchards of stunning apples and pears, which inspired me to make this fruity chutney. As for the BBQ we found to cook the duck on, well, let's just say I wouldn't be surprised to see it putting in an appearance on a French version of Antiques Roadshow.

BBQ DUCK BREAST
WITH APPLE & PEAR CHUTNEY

SERVES TWO

For the chutney
50g demerara sugar
2 pears, peeled, cored
    and cut into large dice
2 apples, cored and cut
    into large dice
1 shallot, finely diced
1 garlic clove, finely chopped
2 star anise
1 teaspoon coriander
    seeds, crushed
1 cinnamon stick
25ml white wine vinegar
100ml apple juice
1 tablespoon chopped tarragon
sea salt and freshly ground
    black pepper

For the duck breast
2 duck breasts, trimmed
1 tablespoon Szechuan
    peppercorns, crushed
2 tablespoons clear honey

Preheat the BBQ: when the coals are silvery in colour, it's ready.

To make the chutney, heat the sugar in a non-stick saucepan over low heat until dissolved. Increase the heat and cook until golden brown and caramelized, about 5 minutes. Add the fruit, shallot, garlic and spices, stir well and then pour in the vinegar and apple juice. Bring to the boil and simmer for 10–15 minutes until thickened and syrupy. Set aside to cool.

Coat the duck breasts in the Szechuan peppercorns and place, skin side down, on the BBQ (or on a hot chargrill pan). Cook for about 2–3 minutes, then turn over and cook for a further 2–3 minutes. Rest the duck for 5 minutes, then brush with the honey and cut into long slices. Serve with a big spoonful of the chutney.

The secret to getting this classic right is the addition of egg yolks and cream at the end – they add an amazing richness and flavour, but if you let the sauce get too hot, the egg yolks will scramble and the sauce will be ruined. This is a delicious dish if you can handle the pressure, though… Just take it easy, keep the heat low and you'll be fine.

CHICKEN BLANQUETTE
WITH HEART-SHAPED CROÛTONS

SERVES FOUR

1 x 1.25–1.5kg chicken
500ml chicken stock
200g baby onions,
  peeled but left whole
250g small button
  mushrooms, cleaned
6 sprigs of tarragon,
  leaves picked
250ml double cream
50g butter
8 slices bread, cut into
  heart-shaped croûtons
1 tablespoon finely
  chopped parsley
5 egg yolks
sea salt and freshly
  ground black pepper

Remove the legs from the chicken and, using a sharp knife, separate the thighs from the drumsticks. Using poultry shears or heavy scissors, lift the breasts from the carcass so that the breast is still attached to the breastbone, then separate the breasts and cut each one in half. (Alternatively, ask your butcher to joint the chicken into 8 pieces for you.)

Place a large saucepan over medium heat. Add the stock, chicken pieces, onions, mushrooms, tarragon and half the cream. Bring to a simmer, then turn the heat down low, cover with a lid and leave to cook for 30 minutes.

Meanwhile, melt the butter in a large frying pan and fry the croûtons on both sides for 1 minute or so until golden brown. Remove from the pan and, while still hot, dip into the parsley. Drain on kitchen paper and set aside.

To finish the blanquette, remove the chicken pieces from the pan and set aside on a warm plate. In a bowl, whisk together the remaining cream and egg yolks, then take the pan off the heat and stir the egg mixture into the sauce. Place the pan back over low heat and stir with a wooden spoon until the sauce thickens, but do not allow it to boil. Pop the chicken back in to warm through, then season with salt and pepper.

Serve on a large platter, garnished with the heart-shaped croûtons.

Pheasants are more popular than I imagined in France, but here in the UK we seem to love game more than most. As pheasant legs can be a bit tough, this dish uses just the breasts.

PHEASANT BREAST
WITH ONION PURÉE & SPRING GREENS

SERVES FOUR

For the onion purée
2 white onions, thinly sliced
1 tablespoon olive oil
300ml double cream
sea salt and freshly ground
  black pepper

For the pheasant
15g unsalted butter
1 tablespoon olive oil
4 pheasant breasts
300ml beef stock
50ml port
2 sprigs of thyme

For the spring greens
2 heads spring greens,
  cut into 1cm strips
30g butter
½ garlic clove, finely sliced

To make the onion purée, place the onions in a saucepan with the olive oil and sweat over low heat, without colouring, for 5 minutes. Add the cream and simmer for 15 minutes until reduced and thick. Place in a blender and purée until very smooth, then season with salt and pepper.

Meanwhile, for the pheasant, heat the butter and olive oil in a large frying pan over medium to high heat. Add the pheasant breasts, skin side down, and fry for 3–4 minutes until golden brown, then turn them over and add the thyme. Cook for another 3–4 minutes, depending on how rare you enjoy your pheasant. Remove the pheasant from the pan and leave to rest in a warm place for 2–3 minutes.

For the spring greens, place a large sauté pan over medium heat. Add the spring greens, butter and garlic and cook, stirring, for 30 seconds. Add 75ml of water and season with salt and plenty of pepper. Stir well and cook for 3–4 minutes until the greens are cooked through.

To serve, place a mound of greens on each plate and sit a pheasant breast on top. Add a spoonful of onion purée alongside.

Now common all over France, confit duck was originally a speciality of Gascony, where it has been made this way for centuries. Traditionally, the duck legs were cured in salt before being slowly cooked in their own fat. The great thing about duck confit is that you can use the fat for seriously good roast potatoes or combine it with some of the shredded meat to make rillettes (see page 30).

CONFIT DUCK
WITH BEAN STEW

SERVES FOUR

For the confit duck legs
4 duck legs
500g duck fat, at room
  temperature
2 bay leaves
small bunch of thyme

For the bean stew
1 large onion, finely diced
4 garlic cloves, crushed
200g chestnut
  mushrooms, sliced
50ml olive oil
400g tin borlotti beans,
  drained and rinsed
400g tin butter beans,
  drained and rinsed
400g tin chopped tomatoes
25g tomato purée
large bunch of flat-leaf
  parsley, leaves picked
  and chopped
sea salt and freshly
  ground black pepper

Preheat the oven to 150°C/300°F/gas mark 2.

For the confit duck, place the duck legs in a large ovenproof dish with a lid and cover with the duck fat. Add the bay leaves and thyme, cover and cook in the oven for 3 hours until the duck is very tender.

For the bean stew, place a large non-stick frying pan over medium heat. Add the olive oil, onions, garlic and mushrooms and cook for 5 minutes until softened. Add the beans and tomatoes and stir in the tomato purée. Bring to the boil and cook over medium heat for another 5 minutes, then stir in the parsley.

Carefully remove the confit duck legs from the dish and drain on kitchen paper. Place a non-stick frying pan over high heat, add the duck legs and fry until browned and crispy. Season with salt and pepper and serve with the bean stew.

We ate so many lovely braised dishes in France that it was difficult to choose just a few to go in the book, but this one made the cut: tarragon is such a classic French herb and the red wine vinegar really lifts the sauce.

BRAISED CHICKEN
WITH RED WINE VINEGAR & TARRAGON

SERVES FOUR

1–2 tablespoons olive oil
1 x 1.25–1.5kg chicken, jointed
   into 8 portions (see page 115)
knob of butter
1 teaspoon tomato purée
2 garlic cloves, finely chopped
50ml red wine vinegar
110ml white wine
500ml chicken stock
2 tomatoes, skinned (see page 14)
1 heaped teaspoon Dijon mustard
250ml whipping cream
1 tablespoon chopped tarragon
sea salt and freshly ground
   black pepper

For the mash
500g potatoes, peeled
   and cut into chunks
125ml double cream
125g unsalted butter, softened

Preheat the oven to 180°C/350°C/gas mark 4.

Heat the olive oil in a large ovenproof frying pan or flameproof casserole over medium to high heat. Season the chicken with salt and pepper and fry to a good golden crisp all over.

Remove the chicken from the pan, then tip out the fat, wipe the pan clean, and add the butter. Stir in the tomato purée and cook over medium heat for 2 minutes, then add the garlic and cook for a further minute. Add the vinegar and reduce until it has all but disappeared. Add the wine and reduce by a third. Pour in the chicken stock and bring to a simmer, then return the chicken to the pan, cover with a lid and transfer to the oven. Cook for 20 minutes or until the chicken is cooked through.

Meanwhile, quarter the tomatoes and scoop out the seeds. Cut the tomato flesh into small dice and set aside.

To make the mash, cook the potatoes in a saucepan of lightly salted water for 15 minutes until tender. Drain and pass through a potato ricer back into the saucepan and stir over low heat to dry out. Gently warm the cream in a small saucepan until just boiling, then remove from the heat. Gradually beat a little butter and then a little of the cream into the mash. Keep adding and beating until the potato is soft and creamy, then season with salt and pepper to taste.

Remove the pan from the oven, lift out the chicken pieces and keep warm while you finish the sauce. Strain the sauce through a sieve into a clean saucepan and bring back to the boil. Whisk in the mustard and cream, then simmer to reduce and thicken slightly. Check the seasoning, then add the diced tomato and tarragon.

Pour the sauce over the chicken and serve with the mash.

Legend is a word that gets used too often, I think, but in the food world the Roux family stand tall. Hard work, skill and dedication have kept them at the top of their game for so many years. This dish is ace. Better still, I cooked it with the legendary Michel Roux Snr himself at his house in France – and even better, he's a great friend. This is one of the best cooking moments I've had on TV since I started this game more than twenty years ago.

BBQ QUAIL
WITH SAUSAGES & CONFIT TOMATOES

SERVES FOUR

For the confit tomatoes
1kg plum tomatoes
2 garlic cloves, thinly sliced
good handful of thyme sprigs
100ml olive oil
2 tablespoons balsamic
  or sherry vinegar
1 tablespoon icing sugar

For the quail and sausages
4 whole quail
4 Toulouse sausages
3 sprigs of thyme, leaves picked
50ml olive oil
1 garlic bulb, cut in half
4 slices sourdough bread
sea salt and freshly ground
  black pepper

For the confit tomatoes, preheat the oven to 110°C/225°F/gas mark ¼. Halve the tomatoes lengthways and place in a roasting tin with the rest of the ingredients. Mix everything together with your hands, then arrange the tomatoes in rows, cut sides up. Cook in the oven for 1 hour, then turn them over and cook for another 1–1½ hours, until very tender and slightly shrivelled. (You only need 10 tomato halves for this recipe, but the rest will keep in the fridge for up to a week and are great in sandwiches and salads.)

For the quail and sausages, preheat the BBQ: when the coals are silvery in colour, it's ready.

Using poultry shears or a heavy knife, cut out the undercarriages of the quail and open out the birds, pressing down with the heel of your hand to flatten (or ask your butcher to spatchcock the quail for you).

Place the sausages on the BBQ and cook, turning occasionally, for about 12–15 minutes until nicely browned and cooked through.

In a small bowl, mix the thyme with the olive oil, then brush the quail with this thyme oil and season with salt and pepper. Place the quail on the BBQ, skin side down, and cook for about 5 minutes, then turn and cook for a further 4–5 minutes. Remove from the BBQ and allow to rest for 5 minutes.

Meanwhile, put 10 confit tomato halves into a small saucepan and warm gently, either on the stovetop or to one side of the BBQ. Rub the cut sides of the garlic over the bread, then grill the bread on the BBQ.

To serve, place the chargrilled bread on a board or serving platter and spoon over the warm confit tomatoes. Lay the quail on the bread, drizzling them with some of the olive oil from the tomatoes. Season with salt and pepper, then scatter the sausages over the top.

Rabbit is found in every butcher's shop up and down France, and of course mustard sauce is the classic accompaniment. This can be made with grainy or smooth mustard – just steer clear of the darker mustards, as these are generally too strong for cooking.

RABBIT
IN MUSTARD SAUCE

SERVES SIX

25ml olive oil
1 rabbit, jointed (ask your
  butcher to do this)
150g baby onions, quartered
2 garlic cloves, finely chopped
4 sprigs of thyme
2 bay leaves
600ml chicken stock
100ml port
4 teaspoons grainy mustard
100ml double cream
sea salt and freshly ground
  black pepper
300g cooked green and
  yellow beans, to serve

Preheat the oven to 180°C/350°F/gas mark 4.

Place a large ovenproof frying pan or flameproof casserole over high heat and add the olive oil. When hot, add the rabbit pieces and sear on all sides, then remove from the pan and set aside on a plate. Add the onions, garlic, thyme and bay leaves to the pan, then pour in the chicken stock and port and bring to the boil. Simmer until reduced by half.

Stir the mustard into the sauce and put the rabbit back in the pan, then cover with a lid and cook in the oven for 1½ hours, or until the rabbit is really tender.

Remove from the oven, stir in the cream and season to taste with salt and pepper. Serve the rabbit with green and yellow beans on the side.

Fruit goes so well with duck, as it cuts through the fattiness of the meat.
If you get a chance on your travels, do try duck magret (breast of duck
raised for foie gras) – the ratio of fat to meat gives it an amazing flavour.

ROAST DUCK
WITH SHERRY VINEGAR & PLUMS

SERVES SIX TO EIGHT

2 x 2kg ducks
2 tablespoons olive oil
4 tablespoons clear honey
handful of thyme sprigs
8 red plums, halved and
   stones removed
1 star anise
1 cinnamon stick
100ml sherry vinegar
sea salt and freshly
   ground black pepper

Preheat the oven to 200°C/400°F/gas mark 6.

Season the ducks with salt and pepper. Place a large frying pan over medium heat and add half of the olive oil, together with the honey and the thyme. Fry the ducks, one at a time, until well browned and glazed, then transfer to a large roasting tin. Roast the ducks in the oven for 1–1½ hours, until the juices run clear from the thickest part of the thigh when pierced with the tip of a knife. Remove the ducks from the oven and leave to rest in a warm place for 15–20 minutes.

Meanwhile, cut the plums into 2cm dice and place in a very hot frying pan with the remaining olive oil. Sauté for 1 minute, then add the star anise and cinnamon stick and cook for 5 minutes. Just as the plums are starting to soften, deglaze the pan with the sherry vinegar and season to taste with salt and pepper.

Serve the ducks with the spiced plums.

This is a true French classic, and one that Keith Floyd loved so much it simply had to be in the book.

COQ AU VIN

SERVES FOUR TO SIX

1 x 1.25–1.5kg chicken
12 garlic cloves, peeled
750ml white wine
12 baby onions, peeled
  but left whole
2 sprigs of thyme
500ml chicken stock
200g bacon lardons
50g butter
300g wild mushrooms
100ml double cream
sea salt and freshly
  ground black pepper

Place the chicken in a large dish with the garlic and wine, cover with cling film and place in the fridge overnight.

Next day, remove the chicken from the fridge and transfer, along with its marinade, to a large sauté pan or flameproof casserole. Add the onions, thyme and stock and bring to the boil, then turn down to a simmer, cover and cook gently for 2 hours.

Remove the chicken and keep in a warm place. Turn up the heat and reduce the cooking liquid to around a quarter of its original volume.

In a large frying pan, melt the butter over medium heat and fry the lardons and mushrooms until crispy, then add to the sauce, together with the cream. Return the chicken to the pan and gently warm through before serving.

VEGETABLES & SALADS

Unusually, we cooked this with horse racing going on in the background, after finding some lovely leeks at the market that morning. With this flavour-packed dressing, leeks vinaigrette is great alongside meat or fish, or simply with a poached egg on top as a dish in its own right.

LEEKS VINAIGRETTE

SERVES SIX

500g baby leeks, trimmed
1 large tablespoon Dijon mustard
50ml white wine vinegar
200ml olive oil
1 small shallot, finely diced
1 garlic clove, crushed
6 sprigs of tarragon

Place the leeks in a large saucepan of lightly salted boiling water and blanch for 2–3 minutes until just soft.

Meanwhile, mix all the other ingredients together in a shallow dish.

Drain the leeks, add to the dish and coat in the vinaigrette while they are still warm, then leave to cool in the dressing. Serve at room temperature.

Celeriac is easy enough to find, and we should use it more often. This is the perfect dish for it, a sort of French coleslaw.

CELERIAC & APPLE RÉMOULADE

1 celeriac
2 Granny Smith apples
1 lemon, juiced
5 tablespoons mayonnaise
1 tablespoon Dijon mustard
small bunch of flat-leaf parsley,
    leaves picked and chopped
sea salt and freshly ground
    black pepper

Use a vegetable peeler or sharp knife to remove the skin from the celeriac. Cut into thin slices and then cut the slices into long matchstick strips as thin as you can make them. Do the same with the apples, discarding the cores.

Mix together the mayonnaise, mustard, lemon juice and parsley, then toss through the celeriac and apple. Season with salt and pepper.

I love the bitterness of chicory, particularly when it's pan-fried. In this salad (pictured over the page) the brioche absorbs these pan juices, so you get all the flavour out of the chicory and sausages, and the pieces of brioche turn into the ultimate croûtons.

TOULOUSE SAUSAGE, CHICORY & BRIOCHE SALAD

SERVES TWO

For the salad
1 tablespoon grapeseed oil
2 Toulouse sausages
2 red chicory
1 yellow chicory
25g caster sugar
2 slices brioche loaf
1 teaspoon capers,
   drained and rinsed
1 lemon, juiced
small bunch of flat-leaf
   parsley, leaves picked
   and roughly chopped
2 soft-boiled eggs, peeled

For the dressing
2 teaspoons Dijon mustard
1 tablespoon sherry vinegar
100ml grapeseed oil
sea salt and freshly ground
   black pepper

For the salad, place a heavy-based frying pan over medium heat and drizzle with the oil. Cut each of the sausages on the diagonal into four, add to the pan and cook until golden brown on all sides and cooked through, about 10–15 minutes.

Cut the chicory into quarters lengthways, sprinkle with the sugar and add to the pan with the sausages, allowing it to brown and caramelize. Remove the sausages and chicory from the pan and set aside.

Tear the brioche into small bite-sized pieces and add to the pan. When the brioche has soaked up the cooking juices and turned golden brown, add the capers, lemon juice and parsley to the pan, turn off the heat and gently toss together, allowing them to warm in the pan.

Meanwhile, to make the dressing, whisk together the mustard, vinegar and oil with a tablespoon of water. Season with salt and pepper.

To serve, scatter the chicory and brioche over the plate, then top with the sausages and pan juices. Spoon over the dressing, then cut the eggs in half and arrange on the salad.

Originally from the historic province of Dauphiné, in the south-east of France, gratin dauphinois is the best potato dish ever when it's cooked well.

GRATIN DAUPHINOIS

SERVES TWO

350g new potatoes, scrubbed
150ml double cream
1 garlic clove, crushed
50g unsalted butter
salt and freshly ground
    black pepper
a few whole chives,
    to garnish (optional)

Preheat the oven to 220°C/425°F/gas mark 7.

Thinly slice the potatoes using a mandoline (or a very sharp knife), being careful of your fingers! Place the potato slices in a small saucepan with the cream, garlic and half of the butter. Season generously and bring to the boil, then reduce the heat and simmer for 4 minutes. Remove from the heat.

Generously butter a gratin dish, then spoon the potatoes and cream into the dish, spreading them out evenly. Dot with the remaining butter and bake for 20–30 minutes until the potatoes are cooked through and golden brown on top. Garnish with chives, if liked, then serve.

I grow globe artichokes at home, so I'm used to preparing and cooking them. But when they're in season, you should give them a try too. Classically they would be boiled and served with a hollandaise sauce, but this barigoule at a wonderful café in south-west France caught my eye.

ARTICHOKES BARIGOULE

SERVES SIX

6 globe artichokes,
   stalks removed
2 carrots, diced
½ celeriac, peeled and diced
3 garlic cloves, smashed
250ml chicken stock
200ml olive oil
175ml white wine
1 tablespoon white wine vinegar
sea salt and freshly ground
   black pepper
crusty bread, to serve

Preheat the oven to 165°C/325°F/gas mark 3.

Sit the artichokes in a large ovenproof dish. Place the carrot, celeriac and garlic around the edges, then pour over the stock, oil, wine and vinegar. Season with salt and pepper, cover with foil and bake for 1 hour or until the vegetables are tender.

Serve warm or cold, with crusty bread.

A green salad is served with most meals in France, and these dressings really liven up a bowl of mixed leaves. Aim for a selection of leaves with different colours and textures, such as frisée, chicory and cos lettuce. The French house dressing comes from one of my French mates, who just happens to be one of the best chefs in the world... Enjoy!

GREEN SALAD DRESSINGS

FRENCH HOUSE DRESSING

MAKES 300ML

15ml clear honey
15ml white balsamic vinegar
250ml vegetable oil
½ small shallot, finely diced
¼ garlic clove, finely sliced
½ teaspoon chopped parsley
½ teaspoon chopped chives
½ teaspoon chopped basil
½ teaspoon thyme leaves
sea salt and freshly ground
   black pepper

In a bowl, whisk together the honey and vinegar, then slowly whisk in the oil. Add the shallot, garlic and herbs, then season to taste and serve. This will keep in a screw-topped jar in the fridge for up to a week.

RED WINE DRESSING

MAKES 150ML

2 teaspoons Dijon mustard
2 tablespoons red wine vinegar
1 egg yolk
4 tablespoons walnut oil
4 tablespoons groundnut oil
sea salt and freshly ground
   black pepper

Whisk together the mustard, vinegar and egg yolk in a bowl. In a separate bowl, mix together the two oils, then slowly and gradually whisk into the mustard and vinegar until emulsified. Season with salt and pepper and the dressing is ready – this one is best used on the day it is made.

BLUE CHEESE DRESSING

MAKES 250ML

½ garlic clove, crushed
50ml white wine vinegar
90g Fourme d'Ambert cheese
   or other mild blue cheese
40g Gorgonzola cheese
65ml buttermilk
50ml sour cream
50g mayonnaise
dash of Worcestershire sauce
dash of Tabasco sauce

Place all the ingredients in a small food processor and blitz until smooth. Use immediately or store in an airtight container in the fridge for up to a week.

A bistro and café classic that just had to be in this book. While others do foam, tinsel and fairy dust, this is a proper plate of food.

SALADE NIÇOISE
WITH GRIDDLED TUNA

SERVES FOUR

For the dressing
100ml olive oil
1 tablespoon Dijon mustard
50ml white wine vinegar
1 shallot, finely diced

For the salad
200g new potatoes, scrubbed
200g green or yellow beans,
   topped and tailed
2 cos lettuces, cut into quarters
200g baby red and yellow plum
   tomatoes, any larger ones
   cut in half
½ red onion, thinly sliced
100g black olives, pitted
50g capers, rinsed and drained
50g anchovies, diced
4 soft-boiled eggs, peeled

For the tuna
1 tablespoon olive oil
4 x 200g tuna steaks
sea salt and freshly ground
   black pepper

To make the dressing, whisk all the ingredients together in a bowl and set aside.

For the salad, bring a large saucepan of water to the boil and cook the potatoes for 10–15 minutes until tender, then drain and cut in half. Blanch the beans for 5 minutes, then drain and immediately plunge into cold water to refresh. Drain well.

Mix the potatoes, beans, lettuce, tomatoes, onion, olives, capers and anchovies together in a large bowl and coat in the dressing. Transfer the salad to a large serving bowl.

For the tuna, heat a griddle pan until hot. Lightly oil the tuna steaks, season with salt and pepper and then cook for 1 minute on each side.

Remove the tuna from the pan and allow to rest for 1 minute before breaking into chunks. Break the eggs in half and tuck into the salad, then top with the tuna and serve.

This classic salad was on the menu at Comptoir du Loup Pendu, a wonderful little place in the Rillieux-la-Pape district of Lyon, where the crew and I stopped off for lunch. Afterwards we got talking to the owner, and he kindly let us cook in his courtyard, while all the patrons sat eating their lunch and watching us intently.

LYONNAISE EGG & BACON SALAD

SERVES TWO

For the salad
1 tablespoon olive oil
4 slices smoked bacon,
   cut into 5cm pieces
2 thick slices of bread,
   torn into cubes
2 eggs
a splash of white wine vinegar
2 handfuls of frisée
2 handfuls of lamb's lettuce
2 chicory, sliced
small bunch of chervil

For the dressing
2 teaspoons Dijon mustard
25ml white wine vinegar
100ml olive oil
½ shallot, finely diced
¼ garlic clove, crushed
sea salt and freshly ground
   black pepper

For the salad, heat the oil in a large non-stick frying pan, and fry the bacon until crispy, then add the cubes of bread and fry until golden, stirring regularly. Remove the croûtons and drain on kitchen paper.

Meanwhile, poach the eggs. Bring a large saucepan of water to the boil and add a teaspoon of salt. Crack each egg into a small cup. Using a whisk, swirl the water and drop an egg into the middle. Turn down the heat and gently simmer for 2–3 minutes. Remove the egg with a slotted spoon and plunge into cold water. Repeat with the remaining egg.

To make the dressing, whisk all the ingredients together in a large bowl. Add the frisée, lamb's lettuce, chicory and chervil and gently toss together.

To serve, pile the salad into two shallow bowls and top with the bacon and croûtons. Plunge the eggs into boiling water for 30 seconds to heat through, then drain and place on top of the salad.

When wild mushrooms are in season, there is little better. They're one of the amazing things you look forward to as a cook, year after year, particularly if you go foraging for them in the woods. Not knowing what you'll find is half the enjoyment... Eating is the other half.

WILD MUSHROOM FRICASSÉE

SERVES FOUR

50g butter
1 tablespoon olive oil
2 shallots, finely chopped
1 garlic clove, finely chopped
50g trompette de mort
  mushrooms, cleaned
  and trimmed
50g chanterelle mushrooms,
  cleaned and trimmed
50g girolles mushrooms,
  cleaned and trimmed
150ml chicken stock
75ml double cream
2 tablespoons finely
  chopped chives
2 tablespoons finely
  chopped chervil
sea salt and freshly
  ground black pepper

Place a large frying pan over low to medium heat. Add the butter, oil, shallots and garlic and sweat for 1–2 minutes until just softened. Add the mushrooms and sauté over medium to high heat for 1 minute.

Pour in the chicken stock and simmer until reduced by about a half, then add the cream and gently warm through.

To finish, season with salt and pepper and stir through the chives and chervil.

DESSERTS & PASTRIES

*When I was a pastry chef, about 25 years ago, I think I weighed nearly
25 stone, mainly because I used to eat two of these every day! Not any more,
but there's still nothing better for an indulgent weekend breakfast.*

PAIN AU CHOCOLAT

MAKES ABOUT
TWENTY-FOUR

500g strong bread flour
2 teaspoons salt
80g caster sugar
10g fast-acting dried yeast
300g cold butter
300g dark chocolate,
  broken into small chunks
1 egg, lightly beaten

Place the flour, salt, sugar and yeast in a large mixing bowl. Using
a wooden spoon, slowly mix in about 400ml lukewarm water, until
the dough becomes pliable. The amount of water required may vary
slightly, depending on the absorbency of the flour. Place the dough
on a lightly floured surface and knead well until it feels elastic, about
5 minutes. Return the dough to the bowl, cover with cling film and
leave in the fridge for 1 hour.

Return the chilled dough to the floured work surface and roll out
into a rectangle measuring about 60cm x 30cm. Using the rolling pin,
flatten the butter into a rectangle about 1cm thick and big enough to
cover two-thirds of the dough. Lay the butter over the dough and fold
the remaining one-third of the dough over the buttered dough. You will
be left with one third of buttered dough. Fold this over so that the dough
is in three layers, with the butter inside. Wrap the dough in cling film
and return to the fridge to chill for a further hour.

Scatter some more flour over the work surface and roll out the dough
to the same-sized rectangle as before. Repeat the folding process and
place the dough back in the fridge for another hour. Repeat this process
twice more before wrapping the dough in cling film and leaving it to
rest overnight in the fridge.

The next day, roll out the dough to approximately 5mm thick, then
cut the dough into 13cm squares – you should get about 24. Place a row
of chocolate chunks on one half of each square, then roll up to enclose
the chocolate filling. Place on two large baking sheets and leave in a
warm place until doubled in size, about 1 hour.

Preheat the oven to 200°C/400°F/gas mark 6. Brush the pain au
chocolat with beaten egg and bake for 15 minutes until golden brown.

I cooked this in one of the most beautiful markets I've ever been to, the famous floating market at L'Isle-sur-la-Sorgue, in Provence. Over the years more and more stalls have sprouted along the river, but the produce, like these sun-ripened peaches and basil, is still exceptional. Keith Floyd made this his home in the latter years of his life and you can see why: amazing food, markets, people and scenery. Oh, and I bought my Floyd tribute Panama hat here, of course. Well I had to, didn't I?

PEACH & BASIL PAIN PERDU

SERVES TWO

100g caster sugar
3 ripe peaches, stones
  removed and flesh cut
  into 8 wedges
15 basil leaves
50ml white wine
25g butter
2 eggs
100ml milk
4 x 2cm slices brioche loaf
100g fromage frais or
  natural yoghurt

Sprinkle half of the sugar into a saucepan and cook over medium heat until the sugar is caramelized and deep golden brown. Add the peaches and let cook for 2–3 minutes before shaking the pan. Scatter over the basil leaves and drizzle in the wine, then cover and cook over low heat for 5 minutes.

Meanwhile, place a large frying pan over medium heat and add the butter. In a shallow bowl, mix together the eggs, milk and the remaining sugar with a fork. Dip the brioche slices into the egg mixture, then fry until golden brown on both sides.

To serve, place the brioche on plates, spoon the peaches and their juices alongside and serve with a spoonful of fromage frais or yoghurt.

A classic found in every French pâtisserie, this wonderfully simple apple tart just had to be in the book.

APPLE TART

SERVES FOUR

1 x 320g ready-made
  puff pastry sheet
1 tablespoon icing sugar
2 tablespoons apricot jam
4 eating apples, cored
  and thinly sliced
vanilla ice cream, to serve

Preheat the oven to 200°C/400°F/gas mark 6. Lightly grease a large baking tray.

On a lightly floured surface, roll out the pastry to a 5mm thickness, then cut out 4 x 15cm circles – use a small plate as a template. Place the pastry circles on the prepared baking tray, then prick all over with a fork and dust with the icing sugar.

Warm the apricot jam in a small saucepan over low heat until thin enough to brush.

Arrange the apples over the pastry in circles and brush with the apricot jam. Bake for 10–12 minutes until golden brown and crisp around the edges.

Serve with vanilla ice cream.

The story goes that the classic apple version of this upside-down tart was accidentally created by the Tatin sisters. But here I've deliberately used pears and rosemary for a twist on the original.

PEAR & ROSEMARY TARTE TATIN

SERVES FOUR

For the rough puff pastry
250g plain flour
½ teaspoon salt
250g cold butter,
  cut into small cubes
125ml ice-cold water

For the pear Tatin
4 pears, peeled, cored
  and cut in half
110g caster sugar
2 vanilla pods, split
  and seeds removed
110g butter
150ml double cream
2 sprigs of rosemary

To serve
vanilla ice cream

To make the rough puff pastry, place the flour and salt in a large mixing bowl. Add the butter and use your fingertips to rub the butter into the flour. When the mixture resembles breadcrumbs, add the cold water, mixing it in with a palette knife. When the dough comes together, turn it out onto a lightly floured surface and knead briefly just until smooth.

Form the dough into a rectangular block (this will make it easier to roll out later), wrap in cling film and refrigerate for 20 minutes. Unwrap the chilled dough and roll out on a lightly floured surface into a rectangle about 40cm x 20cm. Fold one-third of the dough into the centre, then fold the other third over that. Give the pastry a quarter turn and fold in the same way again. Wrap in cling film, refrigerate for 20 minutes, then repeat the rolling out and folding one more time. Wrap in cling film again and refrigerate for 30 minutes before using.

Preheat the oven to 200°C/400°F/gas mark 6.

For the pear Tatin, place the pears, 25g of the sugar and the vanilla seeds in a saucepan. Fill the saucepan with enough water to cover the pears. Bring to a simmer over low heat and cook for 15 minutes, or until the pears are just tender. Drain and pat dry with kitchen paper.

Heat the remaining 85g of sugar in a 24cm ovenproof frying pan over low heat until it has caramelized. Add the butter, cream and rosemary to the pan and heat gently, stirring, until the mixture forms a smooth caramel. Carefully place the pears in the caramel, cut side up, fitting them snugly in the pan.

Roll out the chilled pastry on a lightly floured surface to a 5mm thickness, then cut out a circle slightly larger than the frying pan. Place the pastry over the pears, tucking the edges inside the pan around the pears. Transfer to the oven and bake for 20–25 minutes, or until the pastry is risen, golden brown and cooked through. Remove and set aside to cool for 5–10 minutes.

To serve, carefully invert the tart onto a serving plate. Slice into wedges and top with a scoop of vanilla ice cream.

In the Les Halles de Lyon Paul Bocuse market I had one of the most delicious custard tarts I've ever tasted, made with pistachio nuts and sugar and encased in a kind of big biscuit. I like this even more, though.

BAKED CUSTARD TART
WITH MULLED SPICED PLUMS

SERVES EIGHT TO TEN

For the tart
250g ready-made sweet
   shortcrust pasty
400ml double cream
1 vanilla pod, split and
   seeds scraped
5 egg yolks
1 whole egg
100g caster sugar

For the plums
4 tablespoons caster sugar
50g butter
8–10 dark-skinned plums,
   halved and stones removed
100ml red wine
1 bay leaf
1 cinnamon stick
½ teaspoon freshly
   grated nutmeg
2 cloves
2 star anise

Grease a high-sided 30cm flan tin. Roll out the pastry on a lightly floured surface and use to line the tin, leaving any excess pastry hanging over the edges. Line with greaseproof paper and fill with dried beans or rice, then leave to rest in the fridge for 20–30 minutes.

Preheat the oven to 180°C/350°F/gas mark 4.

Bake the tart shell for 12–15 minutes until the pastry is set. Remove from the oven and take out the greaseproof paper and beans or rice. Using a sharp knife, carefully trim off the excess pastry. Turn the oven down to 130°C/250°F/gas mark 1.

To make the filling, in a small saucepan, bring the cream to the boil with the vanilla pod and seeds, then remove from the heat and leave to infuse for about 20 minutes. Discard the vanilla pod.

Using a wooden spoon, beat the egg yolks and whole eggs together in a bowl with the sugar until smooth. Slowly stir in the infused cream, then pass the custard through a sieve into a jug.

When you're ready to fill the tart, place the tart shell on a baking tray in the oven, then pull the shelf out a little. Pour the filling into the tart shell until it is full to the brim then carefully slide the shelf back and close the oven door. Bake for about 40–50 minutes or until the custard is just set: when you gently shake the tray, the custard should still wobble slightly.

Meanwhile, for the plums, place the sugar and butter in a frying pan over high heat. When bubbling, add the plums, red wine, bay leaf and spices. Reduce the heat and simmer for 10 minutes until the juices have thickened to a syrup, then remove from the heat and leave to cool a little.

Serve the tart in wedges alongside the warm plums.

While we were in the Dordogne, we came across a market in Rouffignac selling the most amazing strawberries, and I couldn't resist buying some to make this dessert. Needless to say, there was also a brass band that just happened to start up in the middle of filming.

INSIDE-OUT TRIFLE MEETS SUMMER PUDDING

SERVES FOUR TO SIX

600g strawberries
50g caster sugar
50ml cold water
12 lemon verbena leaves
500g mascarpone cheese
75ml double cream
drizzle of grapeseed oil
1 brioche loaf

Keep a generous handful of the strawberries whole, with stalks on, to decorate the finished dessert.

Remove the stalks from the rest of the strawberries. Place a saucepan over medium heat and add half of these strawberries to the pan. Sprinkle over the sugar and water and allow to cook for 3–4 minutes until the fruit is soft enough to crush lightly with a fork. Set aside to cool for 10 minutes.

Cut the remaining strawberries in half and place in a bowl, pour over the cooked strawberries in the pan and scatter over the lemon verbena leaves. Mix well and leave to one side.

In a clean bowl, whisk the mascarpone and cream together to form soft but firm peaks.

Brush a bowl or pudding basin with oil, then line with cling film, overlapping it so the whole inside is well covered. Make sure the cling film overhangs the edges of the bowl by about 10cm all around.

Cut the brioche into 1cm-thick slices and use to line the prepared bowl, doing the sides first, then the bottom and slightly overlapping each slice. Gently press two large spoonfuls of the strawberry mix into the base of the mould, then add a couple of spoonfuls of the mascarpone mixture, spreading it flat. Repeat the layers until the bowl is full then top with the remaining brioche slices, completely covering the filling.

Fold over the excess cling film, pressing down gently.

To serve, fold back the cling film, place a serving plate upside down over the bowl and carefully invert onto the plate. Carefully lift the bowl away, holding the edges of the cling film if necessary, to un-mould. Remove the cling film and scatter the reserved strawberries over the top and around the edges.

Try making this cake using different honeys, such as lavender, chestnut or thyme – the flavour of the honey will intensify when the cake is baked.

HONEY CAKE

SERVES EIGHT

For the cake
150g clear honey
150g butter
80g light muscovado sugar
2 eggs, lightly beaten
200g self-raising flour, sieved

For the icing
150g icing sugar
2 tablespoons clear honey

Preheat the oven to 180°C/350°F/gas mark 4. Butter an 18cm round springform cake tin and line the base with baking parchment.

Place the honey, butter and sugar in a large saucepan. Add a tablespoon of water and heat gently until melted. Remove from the heat and let it cool for 5 minutes. Using a wooden spoon, beat in the eggs and flour to make a smooth batter.

Spoon into the prepared tin and bake for 40–45 minutes, until the cake is springy to the touch and is shrinking slightly from the sides of the tin. Remove from the oven and leave to cool slightly in the tin before turning out onto a wire rack.

While the cake is still warm, make the icing. In a bowl, mix together the icing sugar and honey, then gradually add 2–3 tablespoons of hot water, stirring until smooth.

Slide a plate under the wire rack to catch any drips, then trickle the icing over the top of the cake.

The spectacularly situated village of Les Baux-de-Provence is one of the most photographed in France. It has a great restaurant too, the Michelin-starred L'Oustau de Baumanière, where chef Jean-André Charial cooked me an amazing lobster dish. But, chugging back up the hill in the old 2CV, I still couldn't resist stopping at a pâtisserie for one of these huge meringues!

GIANT CHOCOLATE & HAZELNUT MERINGUES

SERVES FIVE TO SIX

For the meringues
5 egg whites
250g caster sugar
1 teaspoon cornflour
100g dark chocolate,
  broken into chunks

For the filling
400ml double cream
100g hazelnuts, toasted
  and chopped

Preheat the oven to 100°C/200°F/gas mark ¼. Line a large baking sheet with baking parchment.

For the meringues, in a really clean, dry bowl of an electric mixer, whisk the egg whites to soft peaks. Gradually whisk in the sugar, a tablespoon at a time, until the whites form stiff peaks. Add the cornflour and whisk again.

Using a large metal spoon, place 10 or 12 large spoonfuls of the meringue on the prepared baking tray. Bake in the oven, on the middle shelf, for 3 hours until dry and crisp. Turn the oven off and leave the meringues inside to cool.

Place the chocolate in a heatproof bowl set over a saucepan of just simmering water – do not let the bottom of the bowl touch the water. Heat gently, stirring, until the chocolate is melted. Remove from the heat and dip the base of each meringue into the melted chocolate. Leave to set on a wire rack with a sheet of baking parchment underneath to catch any drips.

For the filling, whip the cream to soft peaks, then fold through the hazelnuts. Use to sandwich two meringues together just before serving.

Originally created to honour Dame Nellie Melba, this dessert makes the most of peaches at the height of their season – and the peaches in the markets in France were some of the best I've ever seen and tasted.

PEACH MELBA
WITH PISTACHIO, ALMOND & RASPBERRY CARAMEL SAUCE

SERVES TWO

For the peaches
2 peaches
50g unsalted butter, diced

For the sauce
75g caster sugar
1 orange, juiced
25g flaked almonds
25g pistachios
100g raspberries

To serve
300g vanilla ice cream
25g pistachios,
  roughly chopped
25g flaked almonds,
  roughly chopped

Preheat the oven to 200°C/400°F/gas mark 6. Line a small baking tray with baking parchment.

Place the peaches on another baking tray and blowtorch the skin until it is blistered. (Alternatively, blanch the peaches in boiling water for about a minute until the skins split and start to peel away.) Once cool enough to handle, remove the skins. Cut the peaches in half and remove the stones. Place the halves, cut side up, in the prepared baking tray. Dot with the butter and roast in the oven for 15–20 minutes or until the peaches are soft but still holding their shape.

Meanwhile, for the sauce, heat a small frying pan until hot, add the caster sugar and heat gently until it forms a caramel, swirling the pan occasionally to help the sugar dissolve evenly. Add the orange juice (it will spit, so be careful) and swirl to combine. Add the almonds, pistachios and raspberries and heat through for a minute only – you don't want the raspberries to break down. Remove from the heat.

To serve, place the cooked peaches in a shallow serving bowl and pour over the sauce. Serve with the vanilla ice cream and sprinkle with the chopped nuts.

It's not an ice cream, it's not a parfait, but a lovely dessert I used to make when I first worked in France at 14 years old. These frozen soufflés aren't cooked, so they couldn't be simpler to make.

ICED BLACKBERRY SOUFFLÉS

SERVES SIX

200g blackberries
3 large egg whites
100g caster sugar
300ml double cream

Wrap a strip of baking parchment around the outside of six ramekins, ensuring you have at least a 3cm 'collar' at the top. Tie securely with string to hold the parchment in place.

Purée the blackberries in a food processor or blender until smooth.

Using an electric mixer, whisk the egg whites and sugar to firm peaks. In a separate bowl, whip the cream to soft peaks.

Gently fold the blackberry purée, egg whites and cream together using a metal spoon until evenly mixed, then divide between the prepared ramekins and freeze for at least 2 hours.

Remove the soufflés from the freezer, carefully take off the parchment and leave at room temperature for 30 minutes before serving.

Annecy was where I found the most beautiful market I visited on my trip. Even at 7 o'clock in the morning, the place and the food were stunning – and I spotted a French version of my dog Ralph! Annecy also provided the inspiration for this elegant fruit tart.

FRENCH FRUIT TART

SERVES SIX TO EIGHT

1 x 320g ready-made puff
    pastry sheet
1 egg, beaten
85g dark chocolate, broken
    into pieces (optional)
300ml double cream
200ml ready-made
    chilled custard
12 strawberries,
    hulled and halved
150g blueberries
150g raspberries
200g redcurrants
150g seedless black or
    green grapes, halved

Roll out the pastry on a lightly floured surface to a large rectangle, then cut out a 36cm x 20cm rectangle and place on a lightly greased baking tray. Using a sharp knife, score a 2cm frame around the edge, making sure you don't cut the pastry all the way through. Brush the border with beaten egg, taking care not to allow any to dribble down the sides because this will prevent the pastry from rising evenly. Prick the base of the tart (not the border) with a fork, then chill in the fridge for 20 minutes.

Preheat the oven to 200°C/400°F/gas mark 6.

Bake the pastry until golden brown and crisp, about 20–25 minutes. Slide onto a wire rack and leave to cool. Once cooled, gently press the centre of the pastry down to leave the frame around the edge.

Melt the chocolate (if using) in a heatproof bowl set over a saucepan of just simmering water, taking care that the base of the bowl doesn't touch the water. Brush the melted chocolate over the pastry base, keeping clear of the frame. Leave to set.

In a large bowl, whip the cream to soft peaks, then gently fold in the custard. Spoon over the pastry base, spreading it out evenly. Draw shallow lines in the cream mixture to create five sections and arrange the fruit on top so that each section is of a contrasting colour.

This herb is my favourite in my garden at home – it's perfect for infusing custard for crème brûlée and making flavoured teas (if you like that sort of thing). Here the leaves add a gentle citrus note to the meringues, but if you can't get hold of any, a little finely grated lemon zest will do the trick.

LEMON VERBENA MERINGUES
WITH VANILLA CREAM & STRAWBERRIES

SERVES FOUR

For the meringues
6 egg whites
180g icing sugar, sifted
180g caster sugar
a few tiny lemon
  verbena leaves

For the sauce and filling
375g strawberries, hulled
400ml double cream
2 tablespoons icing sugar
1 vanilla pod, split and
  seeds scraped

To garnish
4 sprigs of lemon verbena

Preheat the oven to 100°C/200°F/gas mark ¼. Line a large baking sheet with baking parchment.

To make the lemon verbena meringues, use an electric mixer to whisk the egg whites with the caster sugar to stiff peaks. Add the icing sugar and continue to whisk for 4–6 minutes, or until the meringue is smooth and shiny. Stir in the lemon verbena leaves.

Using two large metal spoons, shape a quenelle of the mixture and place it on the prepared baking sheet. Repeat the process to make seven more meringues, spacing them well apart on the baking sheet. Place the meringues in the oven and cook for 2 hours.

Remove the meringues from the oven and allow to cool slightly before gently easing them from the baking sheet with a palette knife. Transfer to a wire rack and set aside.

Place 250g of the strawberries in a small food processor and blend until smooth, then pass through a sieve into a bowl to remove the seeds. Thinly slice the remaining strawberries.

To make the filling, whip the cream, icing sugar and vanilla seeds together until soft peaks form.

To serve, spoon some of the cream onto the base of half of the meringues, top with a few strawberry slices and sandwich together with the remaining meringues. Garnish with the lemon verbena sprigs and serve the strawberry sauce alongside in a bowl.

I'll never forget cooking this dish on location: it was 34 degrees in the shade, and we were under a beautiful tree by a swimming pool overlooking Saint-Tropez. The other thing I should mention is that the person I was cooking it for was my great friend and three-star Michelin chef, Michel Roux Snr... We were at his house. No pressure, then.

CRÊPES SUZETTE

SERVES TWO

For the crêpes
250g plain flour
2 eggs
2 teaspoons melted butter,
  plus extra for cooking
600ml milk

For the sauce
50g butter
3 oranges, 1 zested and all juiced
1 lemon, zested and juiced
3 tablespoons caster sugar
2 tablespoons Grand Marnier
2 tablespoons Cognac

To make the crêpes, whisk all the ingredients together in a bowl to form a smooth batter. Set aside for at least an hour in a cool place.

Place a small frying pan over medium heat and add a little butter, then a ladleful of batter and swirl to coat the bottom of the pan. Cook for 1–2 minutes until just set, then flip and cook for a further minute until the underneath is lightly browned.

Remove the cooked crêpe from the pan and repeat until all of the batter is used – you should end up with four crêpes. Place layers of baking parchment between the cooked crêpes to stop them sticking together.

For the sauce, place all the ingredients in a large frying pan and bring to the boil, gently shaking the pan to ignite the alcohol. When the flame dies down, fold the crêpes into quarters and nestle them into the pan of sauce. Let them warm through for a few minutes, then dish out.

Although raspberries are available all year round in supermarkets, this luscious raspberry slice is especially good made with fresh, locally grown raspberries at the height of their season. It's also delicious made with strawberries.

RASPBERRY SLICE
WITH RASPBERRY SAUCE

SERVES FOUR TO SIX

1 x 320g ready-made
 puff pastry sheet

For the crème pâtissière
250ml milk, plus
 1 tablespoon extra
1 vanilla pod, split
 and seeds scraped
2 egg yolks
50g icing sugar
10g cornflour
10g plain flour
125ml double cream
1 tablespoon caster sugar

For the raspberry sauce
200g raspberries
2–3 tablespoons icing
 sugar, to taste

To serve
300g raspberries

Preheat the oven to 200°C/400°F/gas mark 6. Lightly grease a large baking sheet.

Lay out the pastry sheet on a lightly floured surface and cut widthways into three rectangles about 22cm x 11cm. Place the pastry rectangles side by side on the prepared baking sheet and dust the tops with the icing sugar. Bake the pastry for 15 minutes, or until golden brown and well risen. Remove from the oven and set aside to cool.

For the crème pâtissière, put the milk in a saucepan, together with the vanilla pod and seeds. Warm over low heat to just below a simmer. In a heatproof bowl, use a wooden spoon to beat the egg yolks, icing sugar, cornflour, plain flour and the extra tablespoon of milk to a thick paste. Gradually whisk in the warmed milk, then pass through a fine sieve back into the saucepan. Cook the crème pâtissière over low heat, whisking constantly, until thickened, then let it bubble for 30 seconds. Remove from the heat and leave to cool completely, covered with a dusting of icing sugar or a layer of cling film to stop a skin forming.

Whip the cream in a large bowl until soft peaks form and then whisk in the caster sugar and keep whisking to stiff peaks. Beat a little of the whipped cream into the cooled crème pâtissière, then gently fold in the remaining cream. Spoon the mixture into a piping bag fitted with a 5mm plain nozzle and chill until needed.

For the raspberry sauce, place the raspberries in a small food processor and blend to a smooth purée. Taste and add icing sugar to sweeten, if needed. Pass the mixture through a fine sieve into a jug.

Place one piece of pastry in the centre of a serving plate and pipe over half of the crème pâtissière in small dots, followed by a third of the raspberries. Repeat these layers, then top with the final piece of pastry and the remaining raspberries. Dust with icing sugar and serve in slices with the raspberry sauce – use a large serrated knife to cut through the flaky pastry layers.

At the Michelin-starred restaurant of the Hostellerie de Plaisance in Saint-Émilion, I ended up making this for staff dinner – I think it was the chef's way of testing me. Or maybe it was just that this much-loved classic French dessert is a staff favourite.

CHOCOLATE MOUSSE

SERVES SIX

200g dark chocolate,
  broken into pieces
3 large eggs, separated
50g caster sugar
softly whipped cream,
  to serve (optional)

Place the chocolate and 120ml of water in a large heatproof bowl set over a pan of just simmering water – do not let the bottom of the bowl touch the water. Heat gently, stirring, until the chocolate is melted.

Remove from the heat and leave to cool slightly, then stir in the egg yolks with a wooden spoon until well combined.

In a large bowl, whisk the egg whites with the sugar until stiff peaks form, then gently fold into the chocolate mixture.

Spoon the mousse into individual dishes and chill for at least 2 hours or overnight. Top with softly whipped cream, if desired.

When made with good-quality cream and vanilla, this is still one of the best desserts you can have. To set the crème, you can either cook it on the stovetop or in the oven, but I find baking it gives a better, creamier texture.

CRÈME BRÛLÉE

SERVES EIGHT

350ml double cream
125ml milk
2 vanilla pods, split
   and seeds scraped
4 eggs
4 egg yolks
130g caster sugar

Preheat the oven to 150°C/325°F/gas mark 3.

In a saucepan, gently warm the cream and milk with the vanilla pods and seeds, then remove from the heat and leave to infuse and cool for about 20 minutes.

In a large bowl, whisk the eggs and egg yolks with 50g of the sugar until smooth. Remove the vanilla pods from the pan, then whisk the infused cream mixture into the egg mixture.

Pour into 8 ramekin dishes until nearly full. Sit the ramekins in a high-sided ovenproof dish and pour in enough warm water to come two-thirds of the way up the ramekins.

Carefully transfer to the oven and cook for 30 minutes until just set. Remove the ramekins from the water bath, leave to cool and then chill in the fridge for an hour.

To serve, sprinkle over the remaining 80g of caster sugar and blowtorch to form a crisp caramel. Alternatively, heat the grill to high and grill until the sugar is crisp and golden.

INDEX

ACKNOWLEDGEMENTS

There are so many people to thank for this book: everyone at ITV, for having faith in me; Poppy Floyd, for offering me the car in the first place; Emma, Andy and all the team at Blue Marlin Television, who travelled with me across France and beyond; and to David and Karen, for handling the logistics. To Pete, for getting the 2CV into the most unlikely places and occasionally halfway up a mountain; to Sam and Chris, for the food; and to Peter, for the amazing photographs, both on location and at the food shoot. To Fiona and everyone at Limelight Management, for keeping me busy; and to Sarah and all at Quadrille, for making such a brilliant book. To all the wonderful people and chefs who generously opened their doors for us to experience true France at its best. But most of all, thanks to Keith: rest in peace, mate – you're a legend.